# First Workshop on Neural Machine Translation 2017

Held at ACL 2017

Vancouver, Canada
4 August 2017

ISBN: 978-1-5108-4582-4

ACL 2017

**The First Workshop on Neural Machine Translation**

**Proceedings of the Workshop**

August 4, 2017
Vancouver, Canada

# Introduction

Welcome to the ACL Workshop on Neural Machine Translation. This is a new annual workshop focusing on Neural Machine Translation (NMT) technology, a simple new architecture for getting machines to learn to translate. Despite being relatively recent, NMT has demonstrated promising results and attracted much interest, achieving state-of-the-art results on a number of shared tasks. This workshop aims to cultivate research in neural machine translation and other aspects of machine translation and multilinguality that utilize neural models.

In this year's workshop we are extremely fortunate to be able to host four invited talks from leading lights in the field, namely: Chris Dyer, Alexander Rush, Kevin Knight and Quoc Le. In addition the workshop will feature a panel discussion to discuss the burning issues in the field.

We received a total of 24 submissions, and accepted 15 for inclusion in the workshop. Due to the large number of invited talks, and to encourage discussion, only the two papers selected for best paper awards will be presented orally, and the remainder will be presented in a single poster session.

We would like to thank all authors for their submissions, and the program committee members for their valuable efforts in reviewing the papers for the workshop. We would also like to thank Google for their generous sponsorship.

**Organizers:**

Minh-Thang Luong, Google Brain
Alexandra Birch, University of Edinburgh
Graham Neubig, Carnegie Mellon University
Andrew Finch, Apple Inc.

**Program Committee:**

Michael Auli, Facebook
Trevor Cohn, University of Melbourne
Kevin Duh, JHU
Long Duong, University of Melbourne
Francisco Guzman, CSRI
Barry Haddow, Edinburgh
Cong Duy Vu Hoang, University of Melbourne
Sébastien Jean, Montreal
Hidetaka Kamigaito, Titech
Yuta Kikuchi, Titech
Kevin Knight, USC/ISI
Lemao Liu, Tencent AI Lab
Shujie Liu, Microsoft
Chris Manning, Stanford
Hideya Mino, NICT
Preslav Nakov, QCRI
Hieu Pham, Google
Abigail See, Stanford
Rico Sennrich, Edinburgh
Kubosawa Shumpei, NICT
Akihiro Tamura, Ehime University
Rui Wang, NICT
Taro Watanabe, Google
Xiaolin Wang, NICT

**Invited Speakers:**

Chris Dyer, Deepmind
Kevin Knight, (USC/ISI)
Quoc Le, Google Brain
Alexander Rush, Harvard

**Panelists:**

Chris Dyer, Deepmind
Kevin Knight, (USC/ISI)
Quoc Le, Google Brain
Alexander Rush, Harvard
Kyunghyun Cho, New York University

# Table of Contents


*An Empirical Study of Adequate Vision Span for Attention-Based Neural Machine Translation*
Raphael Shu and Hideki Nakayama . . . . . . . . . . . . . . . . . . . . . . . . . . . . . . . . . . . . . . . . . . . . . . 1

*Analyzing Neural MT Search and Model Performance*
Jan Niehues, Eunah Cho, Thanh-Le Ha and Alex Waibel . . . . . . . . . . . . . . . . . . . . . . . . . . . . . 11

*Stronger Baselines for Trustable Results in Neural Machine Translation*
Michael Denkowski and Graham Neubig . . . . . . . . . . . . . . . . . . . . . . . . . . . . . . . . . . . . . . . . . . 18

*Six Challenges for Neural Machine Translation*
Philipp Koehn and Rebecca Knowles . . . . . . . . . . . . . . . . . . . . . . . . . . . . . . . . . . . . . . . . . . . . 28

*Cost Weighting for Neural Machine Translation Domain Adaptation*
Boxing Chen, Colin Cherry, George Foster and Samuel Larkin . . . . . . . . . . . . . . . . . . . . . . . . 40

*Detecting Untranslated Content for Neural Machine Translation*
Isao Goto and Hideki Tanaka . . . . . . . . . . . . . . . . . . . . . . . . . . . . . . . . . . . . . . . . . . . . . . . . . . 47

*Beam Search Strategies for Neural Machine Translation*
Markus Freitag and Yaser Al-Onaizan . . . . . . . . . . . . . . . . . . . . . . . . . . . . . . . . . . . . . . . . . . . 56

*An Empirical Study of Mini-Batch Creation Strategies for Neural Machine Translation*
Makoto Morishita, Yusuke Oda, Graham Neubig, Koichiro Yoshino, Katsuhito Sudoh and Satoshi
Nakamura . . . . . . . . . . . . . . . . . . . . . . . . . . . . . . . . . . . . . . . . . . . . . . . . . . . . . . . . . . . . . . . . . . 61

*Detecting Cross-Lingual Semantic Divergence for Neural Machine Translation*
Marine Carpuat, Yogarshi Vyas and Xing Niu . . . . . . . . . . . . . . . . . . . . . . . . . . . . . . . . . . . . 69

# Workshop Program

**Friday, August 4, 2017**

**Session 1**

| | |
|---|---|
| **09.30—09.40** | ***Welcome and Opening Remarks*** |
| **09.40—10.30** | ***Keynote - Chris Dyer*** |

*10.30—11.00 Coffee Break*

**Session 2**

| | |
|---|---|
| **11.00—11.50** | ***Keynote - Alexander Rush*** |
| **11.50–12.20** | ***Best Paper Session*** |

*12.20—13.40 Lunch Break*

**Session 3**

| | |
|---|---|
| **13.40—14.30** | ***Keynote - Kevin Knight*** |
| **14.30—15.20** | ***Keynote - Quoc Le*** |

**Session 4**

15.20—
15.30
    *Poster Session*

*An Empirical Study of Adequate Vision Span for Attention-Based Neural Machine Translation*
Raphael Shu and Hideki Nakayama

*Analyzing Neural MT Search and Model Performance*
Jan Niehues, Eunah Cho, Thanh-Le Ha and Alex Waibel

*Stronger Baselines for Trustable Results in Neural Machine Translation*
Michael Denkowski and Graham Neubig

*Six Challenges for Neural Machine Translation*
Philipp Koehn and Rebecca Knowles

*Cost Weighting for Neural Machine Translation Domain Adaptation*
Boxing Chen, Colin Cherry, George Foster and Samuel Larkin

*Detecting Untranslated Content for Neural Machine Translation*
Isao Goto and Hideki Tanaka

*Beam Search Strategies for Neural Machine Translation*
Markus Freitag and Yaser Al-Onaizan

*An Empirical Study of Mini-Batch Creation Strategies for Neural Machine Translation*
Makoto Morishita, Yusuke Oda, Graham Neubig, Koichiro Yoshino, Katsuhito Sudoh and Satoshi Nakamura

*Detecting Cross-Lingual Semantic Divergence for Neural Machine Translation*
Marine Carpuat, Yogarshi Vyas and Xing Niu

*Domain Aware Neural Dialogue System (extended abstract)*
Sajal Choudhary, Prerna Srivastava, Joao Sedoc and Lyle Ungar

*Interactive Beam Search for Visualizing Neural Machine Translation (extended abstract)*
Jaesong Lee, JoongHwi Shin and Jun-Seok Kim

*Graph Convolutional Encoders for Syntax-aware Neural Machine Translation (extended abstract)*
Joost Bastings, Ivan Titov, Wilker Aziz, Diego Marcheggiani and Khalil Sima'an

*Towards String-to-Tree Neural Machine Translation (cross-submission)*
Roee Aharoni and Yoav Goldberg

*What do Neural Machine Translation Models Learn about Morphology? (cross-submission)*
Yonatan Belinkov, Nadir Durrani, Fahim Dalvi, Hassan Sajjad and James Glass

*Trainable Greedy Decoding for Neural Machine Translation (cross-submission)*
Jiatao Gu, Kyunghyun Cho and Victor O.K. Li

**15.30—
16.10**     ***Poster Session (continued) and Coffee Break***

**Session 5**

**16.10—
17.30**     ***Panel Discussion***

*17.30—17.40 Closing Remarks*

# An Empirical Study of Adequate Vision Span for Attention-Based Neural Machine Translation

**Raphael Shu, Hideki Nakayama**

shu@nlab.ci.i.u-tokyo.ac.jp, nakayama@ci.i.u-tokyo.ac.jp
The University of Tokyo

## Abstract

Recently, the attention mechanism plays a key role to achieve high performance for Neural Machine Translation models. However, as it computes a score function for the encoder states in all positions at each decoding step, the attention model greatly increases the computational complexity. In this paper, we investigate the adequate vision span of attention models in the context of machine translation, by proposing a novel attention framework that is capable of reducing redundant score computation dynamically. The term "vision span" means a window of the encoder states considered by the attention model in one step. In our experiments, we found that the average window size of vision span can be reduced by over 50% with modest loss in accuracy on English-Japanese and German-English translation tasks.

## 1 Introduction

In recent years, recurrent neural networks have been successfully applied in machine translation. In many major language pairs, Neural Machine Translation (NMT) has already outperformed conventional Statistical Machine Translation (SMT) models (Luong et al., 2015b; Wu et al., 2016).

NMT models are generally composed of an encoder and a decoder, which is also known as encoder-decoder framework (Sutskever et al., 2014). The encoder creates a vector representation of the input sentence, whereas the decoder generates the translation from this single vector. This simple encoder-decoder model suffers from a long backpropagation path; thus, adversely affected by long input sequences.

In recent NMT models, soft attention mechanism (Bahdanau et al., 2014) has been a key extension to ensure high performance. In each decoding step, the attention model computes alignment weights for all the encoder states. Then a context vector, which is a weighted summarization of the encoder states is computed and fed into the decoder as input. In contrast to the aforementioned simple encoder-decoder model, the attention mechanism can greatly shorten the backpropagation path.

Although the attention mechanism provides NMT models with a boost in performance, it also significantly increases the computational burden. As the attention model has to compute the alignment weights for all the encoder states in each step, the decoding process becomes time-consuming. Even worse, recent researches in NMT prefer to separate the texts into subwords (Sennrich et al., 2016) or even characters (Chung et al., 2016), which means massive encoder states have to be considered in the attention model at each step, thereby resulting in increasing computational cost. On the other hand, the attention mechanism is becoming more complicated. For example, the NMT model with recurrent attention modeling (Yang et al., 2016) maintains a dynamic memory of attentions for every encoder states, which is updated in each decoding step.

In this paper, we study the adequate *vision span* in the context of machine translation. Here, the term "vision span" means a window of encoder states considered by the attention model in one step. We examine the minimum window size of an attention model have to consider in each step while maintaining the translation quality. For this purpose, we propose a novel attention framework which we refer to as Flexible Attention in this paper. The proposed attention framework tracks the center of attention in each decoding step, and pre-



*Proceedings of the First Workshop on Neural Machine Translation*, pages 1–10,
Vancouver, Canada, August 4, 2017. ©2017 Association for Computational Linguistics

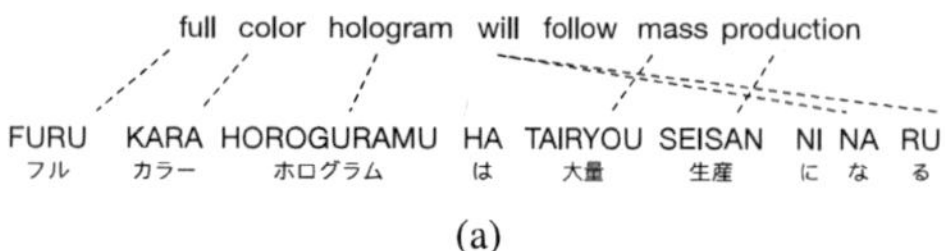


(a)

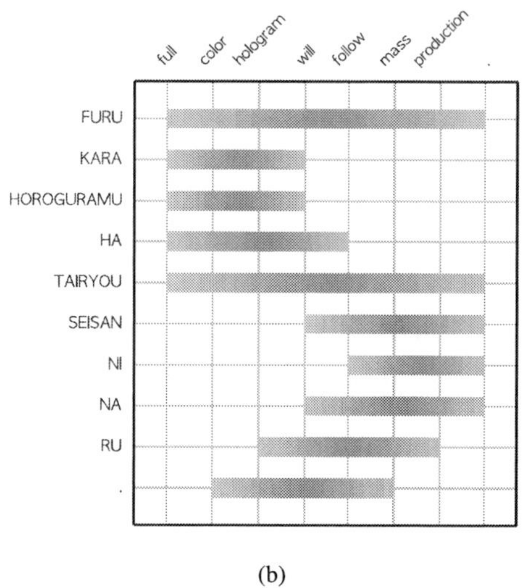


(b)

Figure 1: (a) An example English-Japanese sentence pair with long-range reordering (b) The vision span predicted by the proposed Flexible Attention at each step in English-Japanese translation task

dict an adequate vision span for the next step. In the test time, the encoder states outside of this range are omitted in the computation of score function.

Our proposed attention framework is based on simple intuition. For most language pairs, the translations of words inside a phrase usually remain together. Even the translation of a small chunk usually does not mix with the translation of other words. Hence, information about distant words is basically unnecessary when translating locally. Therefore, we argue that computing the attention over all positions in each step is redundant. However, attending to distant positions remains important when dealing with long-range reordering. In Figure 1(a), we show an example sentence pair with long-range reordering, where the positions of the first three words have monotone alignments, but the fourth word is aligned to distant target positions. If we can predict whether the next word to translate is in a local position, the amount of redundant computation in the attention model can be safely reduced by controlling

the window size of vision span dynamically. This motivated us to propose a flexible attention framework which predicts the minimum required vision span according to the context (See Figure 1(b)).

We evaluated our proposed Flexible Attention by comparing with the conventional attention mechanism, and Local Attention (Luong et al., 2015a) which puts attention on a fixed-size window. We focus on comparing the minimum window size of vision span these models can achieve without hurting the performance too much. Note that as the window size determines the number of times the score function is evaluated, reducing the window size leads to the reduction of score computation. We select English-Japanese and German-English language pairs for evaluation as they consi st of languages with different word orders, which means the attention model cannot simply look at a local range constantly and translate monotonically. Through empirical evaluation, we found with Flexible Attention, the average window size is reduced by 56% for English-Japanese task and 64% for German-English task, with modest loss of accuracy. The reduction rate also achieves 46% for character-based NMT models.

Our contributions can be summarized as three folds:

1. We empirically confirmed that the conventional attention mechanism performs a significant amount of redundant computation. Although attending globally is necessary when dealing with long-range reordering, a small vision span is sufficient when translating locally. The results may provide insights for future research on more efficient attention-based NMT models.

2. The proposed Flexible Attention provides a general framework for reducing the amount of score computation according to the context, which can be combined with other expensive attention models of which computing for all positions in each step is costly.

3. We found that reducing the amount of computation in the attention model can benefit the decoding speed on CPU, but not GPU.

## 2 Attention Mechanism in NMT

Although the network architectures of NMT models differ in various respects, they generally follow the encoder-decoder framework. In Bahdanau et al. (2014), a bidirectional recurrent neural network is used as the encoder, which accepts the embeddings of input words. The hidden states $\bar{h}_1, ..., \bar{h}_S$ of the encoder are then used in the decoding phase. Basically, the decoder is composed of a recurrent neural network (RNN). The decoder RNN computes the next state based on the embedding of the previously generated word, and a context vector given by the attention mechanism. Finally, the probabilities of output words in each time step are predicted based on the decoder states $h_1, ..., h_N$.

The soft attention mechanism (Karol et al., 2015) is introduced to NMT in Bahdanau et al. (2014), which computes a weighted summarization of all encoder states in each decoding step, to obtain the context vector:

$$c_t = \sum_s a_t(s)\bar{h}_s, \qquad (1)$$

where $\bar{h}_s$ is the $s$-th encoder state, $a_t(s)$ is the alignment weight of $\bar{h}_s$ in decoding step $t$. The calculation of $a_t(s)$ is given by the softmax of the weight scores:

$$a_t(s) = \frac{\exp(\text{score}(h_{t-1}, \bar{h}_s))}{\sum_{s'} \exp(\text{score}(h_{t-1}, \bar{h}_{s'}))}. \qquad (2)$$

The unnormalized weight scores are computed with a score function, defined as[1]:

$$\text{score}(h_{t-1}, \bar{h}_s) = v_a^\top \tanh(W_a[h_{t-1}; \bar{h}_s]), \qquad (3)$$

where $v_a$ and $W_a$ are the parameters of the score function, $[h_{t-1}; \bar{h}_s]$ is a concatenation of the decoder state in the previous step and an encoder state. Intuitively, the alignment weight indicates whether an encoder state is valuable for generating the next output word. Note that many discussions on alternative ways for computing the score function can be found in Luong et al. (2015a).

## 3  Flexible Attention

In this section, we present our main idea for reducing the window size of vision span. In contrast to

conventional attention models, we track the center of attention in each decoding step with

$$p_t = \sum_s a_t(s) \cdot s. \qquad (4)$$

The value of $p_t$ provides an approximate focus of attention in time step $t$. Then we penalize the alignment weights for the encoder states distant from $p_{t-1}$, which is the focus in the previous step. This is achieved by a position-based penalty function:

$$\text{penalty}(s) = g(t)d(s, p_{t-1}), \qquad (5)$$

where $g(t)$ is a *sigmoid* function that adjusts the strength of the penalty dynamically based on the context in step $t$. $d(s, p_{t-1})$ provides the distance between position $s$ and the previous focus $p_{t-1}$, which is defined as:

$$d(s, p_{t-1}) = \frac{1}{2\sigma^2}(s - p_{t-1})^2. \qquad (6)$$

Hence, distant positions attract exponentially large penalties. The denominator $2\sigma^2$, which is a hyperparameter, controls the maximum of penalty when $g(t)$ outputs 1.

The position-based penalty function is finally integrated into the computation of the alignment weights as:

$$a_t(s) =$$
$$\frac{\exp(\text{score}(h_{t-1}, \bar{h}_s) - \text{penalty}(s))}{\sum_{s'} \exp(\text{score}(h_{t-1}, \bar{h}_{s'}) - \text{penalty}(s'))}, \qquad (7)$$

where the penalty function acts as a second score function that penalize encoder states only by their positions. When $g(t)$ outputs zero, the penalty function will have no effects on alignment weights. Note that the use of distance-based penalties here is similar in appearance to Local Attention (local-p) proposed in Luong et al. (2015a). The difference is that Local Attention predicts the center of attention in each step and attends to a fixed window. Further discussion will be given later in Section 4.

In this paper, the strength function $g(t)$ in Equation 5 is defined as:

$$g(t) = \text{sigmoid}(v_g^\top \tanh(W_g[h_{t-1}; i_t]) + b_g), \qquad (8)$$

where $v_g$, $W_g$ and $b_g$ are parameters. We refer to this attention framework as Flexible Attention in

---

[1] In the original paper (Bahdanau et al., 2014), the equation of the score function is a sum. Here, we use a concatenation in Equation 3 in order to align with (Luong et al., 2015a), which is an equivalent form of the original equation.

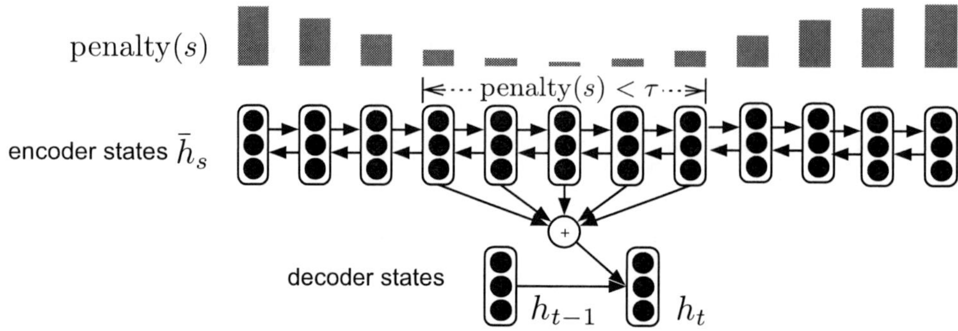


Figure 2: Illustration of the way that Flexible Attention reduces the window of vision span. In each decoding step, only a portion of the encoder states are selected by the position-based penalty function to compute the alignment weights.

this paper, as the window of effective attention is adjusted by $g(t)$ in according to the context.

Intuitively, when the model is translating inside a phrase, the alignment weights for distant positions can be safely penalized by letting $g(t)$ output a high value. If the next word is expected to be translated from a new phrase, $g(t)$ shall output a low value to allow attending to any position. Actually, the selected output word in the previous step can greatly influence this decision, as selection of the output word can determine whether the translation of a phrase is complete. Therefore, the embedding of the feedback word $i_t$ is put into the equation.

### 3.1 Reducing Window Size of Vision Span

As we can see from Equation 7, if a position is heavily penalized, then it will be assigned a low attention probability regardless of the value of the score function. In the test time, we can set a threshold $\tau$, and only compute the score function for positions with penalties lower than $\tau$. Figure 2 provides an illustration of the selection process. The selected range can be obtained by solving $penalty(s) < \tau$, which gives $s \in \left( p_{t-1} - \sigma\sqrt{2\tau/g(t)}, \ p_{t-1} + \sigma\sqrt{2\tau/g(t)} \right)$.

Because the strength term $g(t)$ in Equation 5 only needs to be computed once in each step, the computational cost of the penalty function does not increase as the input length increases. By utilizing the penalty values to omit computation of the score function, the totally computational cost can be reduced.

Although a low threshold would lead to further reduction of the window size of vision span, the performance degrades as information from the

source side will be greatly limited. In practice, we can find a good threshold to balance the tradeoff of performance and computational cost on a validation dataset.

### 3.2 Fine-tuning for Better Performance

In order to further narrow down the vision span, we want $g(t)$ to output a large value to clearly differentiate valuable encoder states from other states encoder based on their positions. Thus, we can further fine-tune our model to encourage it to decode using larger penalties with the following loss function:

$$J = \sum_{i=1}^{D} -\log p(y^{(i)}|x^{(i)}) - \beta\frac{1}{T}\sum_{t=1}^{T} g(t)^{(i)}, \quad (9)$$

where $\beta$ is a hyperparameter to control the balance of cross-entropy and the average strength of penalty. In our experiments, we tested $\beta$ among $(0.1, 0.001, 0.0001)$ on a development data and found that setting $\beta$ to $0.1$ and fine-tuning for one epoch works well. If we train the model with this loss function from the beginning, as the right part of the loss function is easier to be optimized, the value of $g(t)$ saturates quickly, which slows down the training process.

## 4 Related Work

To the best of our knowledge, only a limited number of related studies aimed to reduce the computational cost of the attention mechanism. Local Attention, which was proposed in Luong et al. (2015a), limited the range of attention to a fixed window size. In Local Attention (local-p), the center of attention $p_t$ is *predicted* in each time step $t$:

$$p_t = S \cdot \text{sigmoid}(\boldsymbol{v}_{\boldsymbol{p}}^{\top} \tanh(\boldsymbol{W_p h_t})) \,, \qquad (10)$$

where $S$ is the length of the input sequence. Finally, the alignment weights are computed by:

$$\begin{aligned}
a_t'(s) &= a_t(s) \exp\left(-\frac{(s - p_t)^2}{2\sigma^2}\right) \\
&= \frac{exp(\text{score}(\boldsymbol{h_{t-1}}, \bar{\boldsymbol{h}}_s))}{\sum_{s'} exp(\text{score}(\boldsymbol{h_{t-1}}, \bar{\boldsymbol{h}}_{s'}))} \exp\left(-\frac{(s - p_t)^2}{2\sigma^2}\right),
\end{aligned}$$
$$(11)$$

where $\sigma$ is a hyperparameter determined by $\sigma = D/2$, where $D$ is a half of the window size. Local Attention only computes attention within the window $[p_t - D, p_t + D]$. In their work, the hyperparameter $D$ is empirically set to $D = 10$ for the English-German translation task, which means a window of 21 words.

Our proposed attention model differs from Local Attention in two key points: (1) our proposed attention model does not predict the fixation of attention but tracks it in each step (2) the position-based penalty in our attention model is adjusted flexibly rather than remaining fixed. Note that in Equation 11 of Local Attention, the penalty term is applied outside the softmax function. In contrast, we integrate the penalty term with the score function (Eq. 7), such that the final probabilities still add up to 1.

Recently, a "cheap" linear model (de Brébisson and Vincent, 2016) is proposed to replace the attention mechanism with a low-complexity function. This cheap linear attention mechanism achieves an accuracy in the middle of Global Attention and a non-attention model on a question-answering dataset. This approach can be considered as another interesting way to balance the performance and computational complexity in sequence-generation tasks.

## 5  Experiments

In this section, we focus on evaluating our proposed attention models by measuring the minimum average window size of vision span it can achieve with a modest performance loss[2]. In de-

tail, we measure the average number of the encoder states considered when computing the score function in Equation 3. Note that as we decode using Beam Search algorithm (Sutskever et al., 2014) , the value of window size is further averaged over the number of hypotheses considered in each step. For the conventional attention mechanism, as all positions have to be considered in each step, the average window size equals to the average sentence length of the testing data. Following Luong et al. (2015a), we refer to the conventional attention mechanism as Global Attention in experiments.

### 5.1  Experimental Settings

We evaluate our models on English-Japanese and German-English translation task. As translating these language pairs requires long-range reordering, the proposed Flexible Attention has to correctly predict when the reordering happens and look at distant positions when necessary. The training data of En-Ja task is based on ASPEC parallel corpus (Nakazawa et al., 2016), which contains 3M sentence pairs, whereas the test data contains 1812 sentences, which have 24.4 words on average. We select 1.5M sentence pairs according to the automatically calculated matching scores, which are provided along with the ASPEC corpus. For De-En task, we use the WMT'15 training data consisting of 4.5M sentence pairs. The WMT'15 test data (newstest2015) contains 2169 pairs, which have 20.7 words on average.

We preprocess the En-Ja corpus with "tokenizer.perl" for English side, and Kytea tokenizer (Neubig et al., 2011) for Japanese side. The preprocessing procedure for De-En corpus is similar to Li et al. (2014), except we did not filter sentence pairs with language detection.

The vocabulary size are cropped to 80k and 40k for En-Ja NMT models, whereas 50k for De-En NMT models. The OOV words are replaced with a "UNK" symbol. Long sentences with more than 50 words on either the source or target side are removed from the training set, resulting in 1.3M and 3.8M training pairs for En-Ja and De-En task respectively. We use mini-batch in our training procedure, where each batch contains 64 data samples. All sentence pairs are firstly sorted according to their length before we group them into batches. After which, the order of the mini-batches is shuffled.

---

[2]In our experiments, we try to limit the performance loss to be lower than 0.5 development BLEU. As the threshold $\tau$ is selected using a development corpus, the performance on test data is not ensured.

| Model | English-Japanese | | | German-English | |
|---|---|---|---|---|---|
| | window (words) | BLEU(%) | RIBES | window (words) | BLEU(%) |
| Global Attention baseline | 24.4 | 34.87 | 0.810 | 20.7 | 20.62 |
| Local Attention baseline | 18.4 | 34.52 | 0.809 | 15.7 | 21.09 |
| Flexible Attention ($\tau=\infty$) | 24.4 | 35.01 | 0.814 | 20.7 | 21.31 |
| Flexible Attention ($\tau=1.2$) | 16.4 | 34.90 | 0.812 | 7.8 | 21.11 |
| + fine-tuning ($\tau=1.2$) | **10.7** | 34.78 | 0.807 | **7.4** | 20.79 |

Table 1: Evaluation results on English-Japanese and German-English translation task. This table provides a comparison of the minimum window size of vision span the models can achieve with a modest loss of accuracy.

We adopt the network architecture described in Bahdanau et al. (2014) and set it as our baseline model. The size of word embeddings is 1000 for both languages. For the encoder, we use a bi-directional RNN composed of two LSTMs with 1000 units. For the decoder, we use a one-layer LSTM with 1000 units, where the input in each step is a concatenated vector of the embedding of the previous output $i_t$ and the context vector $c_t$ given by attention mechanism. Before the final softmax layer, we insert a fully-connected layer with 600 units to reduce the number of connections in the output layer.

For our proposed models, we empirically select $\sigma$ in Equation 6 from $(\frac{3}{2}, \frac{10}{2}, \frac{15}{2}, \frac{20}{2})$ on a development corpus. In our experiments, we found the attention models give the best trade-off between the window size and accuracy when $\sigma = 1.5$. Note that the value of $\sigma$ only determines the maximum of penalty when $g(t)$ outputs 1, but does not results in a fixed window size.

The NMT models are trained using Adam optimizer (Kingma and Ba, 2014) with an initial learning rate of 0.0001. We train the model for six epochs and start to halve the learning rate from the beginning of the fourth epoch. The maximum norm of the gradients is clipped to 3. Final parameters are selected by the smoothed BLEU (Lin and Och, 2004) on validation set. During test time, we use beam search with a beam size of 20.

In En-Ja task, we evaluate our implemented NMT models with BLEU and RIBES (Isozaki et al., 2010), in order to align with other researches on the same dataset. The results are reported following standard post-processing procedures[3]. For

De-En task, we report *tokenized* BLEU [4].

## 5.2 Evaluations of Flexible Attention

We evaluate the attention models to determine the minimum window size they can achieve with a modest loss of accuracy (0.5 development BLEU) compared to Flexible Attention with $\tau = \infty$. The results we obtained are summarized in Table 1. The scores of Global Attention (conventional attention model) and Local Attention (Luong et al., 2015a) are listed for comparison. For Local Attention, we found a window size of 21 ($D = 10$) gives the best performance for En-Ja and De-En tasks. In this setting, Local Attention achieves an average window of 18.4 words in En-Ja task and 15.7 words in De-En task, as some sentences in the test corpus have fewer than 21 words.

For Flexible Attention, we search a good $\tau$ among $(0.8, 1.0, 1.2, 1.4, 1.6)$ on a development corpus so that the development BLEU(%) does not degrade more than 0.5 compared to $\tau = \infty$. Finally, $\tau = 1.2$ is selected for both language pairs in our experiments.

We can see from the results that Flexible Attention can achieve comparable scores even consider only half of the encoder states in each step. After fine-tuning, our proposed attention model further reduces 56% of the vision span for En-Ja task and 64% for De-En task. The high reduction rate confirms that the conventional attention model performs massive redundant computation. With Flexible Attention, redundant score computation can be efficiently cut down according to the context. Interestingly, the NMT models using Flexible Attention without the threshold improves the translation accuracy by a small margin, which may indi-

---

[3]We report the scores using Kytea tokenizer. The post-processing procedure for evaluation is described in `http://lotus.kuee.kyoto-u.ac.jp/WAT/evaluation/`

[4]The scores are produced by tokenizing with "tokenizer.perl" and evaluating with "multi-bleu.perl".

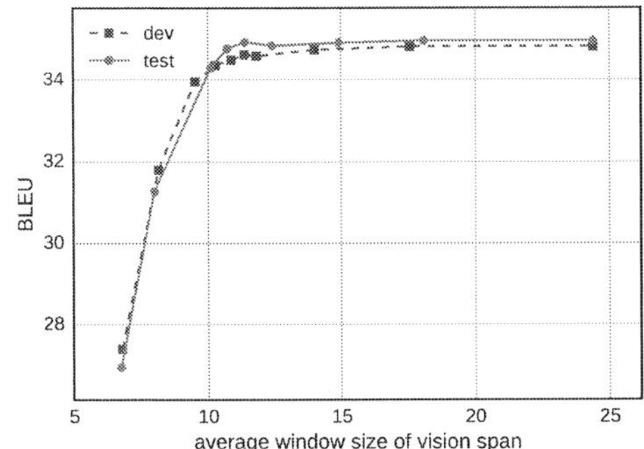

Figure 3: Trade off between window size and performance on the development and test data of English-Japanese tanslation task

cates that the quality of attention is improved.

### 5.3 Trade-off between Window Size and Accuracy

In order to figure out the relation between accuracy and the window size of vision span, we plot out the curve of the trade-off between BLEU score and average window size on En-Ja task, which is shown in Figure 3.

The data points are collected by testing different thresholds [5] with the fine-tuned Flexible Attention model. Interestingly, the NMT model with our proposed Flexible Attention suffers almost no loss in accuracy even the computations are reduced by half. Further trails to reduce the window size beneath 10 words will result in drastically degradation in performance.

### 5.4 Effects on Character-level Attention

| Model | window | BLEU | RIBES |
|---|---|---|---|
| Global Attention baseline | 144.9 | 26.18 | 0.767 |
| Flexible Attention ($\tau=\infty$) | 144.9 | 26.68 | 0.763 |
| Flexible Attention ($\tau=1.0$) | 80.4 | 26.18 | 0.757 |
| + fine-tuning ($\tau=1.0$) | **77.4** | 26.23 | 0.757 |

Table 2: Evaluation results with character-based English-Japanese NMT models

In order to examine the effects of Flexible Attention on extremely long character-level inputs, we also conducted experiments on character-based NMT models. We adopt the same network architecture as word-based models in the English-Japanese task, unless the sentences in both sides are tokenized into characters. We keep 100 most frequent types of character for the English side and 3000 types for the Japanese side. The embedding size is set to 100 for both sides. In order to train the models faster, all LSTMs in this experiment have 500 hidden units. The character-based models are trained 20 epochs with Adam optimizer with an initial learning rate of 0.0001. The learning rate begins to halve from 18-th epoch. After fine-tuning the model with the same hyperparameter ($\beta = 0.1$), we selected the threshold to be $\tau = 1.0$ in the same manner as the word-level experiment. We did not evaluate Local Attention in this experiment as selecting a proper fixed window size is time-consuming when the length of input sequence is extremely long.

The experimental results of character-based models are summarized in Table 2. Note that although the performance of character-based models can not compete with word-based model, the focus of this experiment is to examine the effects in terms of the reduction of the window size of vision span. For this dataset, the character-level tokenization will increase the length of input sequences by 6x on average. In this setting, the fine-tuned Flexible Attention model can achieve a reduction rate of 46% of the vision span. The results indicate that Flexible Attention can automatically adapt to the type of training data and learn to control the strength of penalty properly.

### 5.5 Impact on Real Decoding Speed

In this section, we examine the impact of the reduction of score computation in terms of real decoding speed. We compare the fine-tuned Flexible Attention ($\tau = 1.0$) with the conventional Global Attention on the English-Japanese dataset with character-level tokenization. [6]

We decode 5,000 sentences in the dataset and report the averaged decoding time on both GPU [7] and CPU [8]. For each sequence, the dot production with $\bar{h}_s$ in the score function (Eq. 3) is precomputed and cached before decoding. As differ-

---

[5] In detail, the data points in the plot is based on the thresholds in $(0.3, 0.5, 0.8, 1.0, 1.2, 1.4, 1.6, 5.0, 8.0, 999)$.

[6] For word-level tasks, as the "giant" output layer has large impact on decoding time, we selected the character-level task to measure real decoding speed.

[7] NVIDIA GeForce GTX TITAN X.

[8] Intel Core[TM] i7-5960X CPU @ 3.00GHz, single core. The implementation uses Theano with openblas as numpy backend.

ent attention models will produce different numbers of output tokens for a same input, that the decoding time will be influenced by different computation steps of the decoder LSTM. In order to fairly compare the decoding time, we force the decoder to use the tokens in the reference as feedbacks. Thus, the number of decoding steps remains the same for both models.

| Model | avg. time (GPU) | avg. time (CPU) |
|---|---|---|
| Global Attention | 123ms | 751ms |
| Flexible Attention | 136ms | 677ms |

Table 3: Average decoding time for one sentence on the English-Japanese dataset with character-level tokenization

As shown in Table 3, reducing the amount of computation in attention model is shown to benefit the decoding speed on CPU. However, applying Flexible Attention slows down the decoding speed on GPU. This is potentially due to the overhead of computing the strength of penalty in Equation 8.

For the CPU-based decoding, after profiling our Theano code, we found that the output layer is the main bottleneck, which accounts for 58% of the computation time. In a recent paper (L'Hostis et al., 2016), the authors show that CPU decoding time can be reduced by 90% by reducing the computation of the output layer, resulting in just over 140ms per sentence. Our proposed attention model has the potential to be combined with their method to further reduce the decoding time on CPU.

As the score function we use in this paper has relatively low computation cost, the difference of real decoding speed is expected to be enlarged with more complicated attention models, such as Recurrent Attention (Yang et al., 2016) and Neural Tensor Network (Socher et al., 2013).

### 5.6 Qualitative Analysis of Flexible Attention

In order to inspect the behaviour of the penalty function in Equation 7, we let the NMT model translate the sentence in Figure 1(a) and record the word positions the attention model considers in each step. The vision span predicted by Flexible Attention is visionized in Figure 1(b).

We can see that the value of $g(t)$ changes dynamically in different context, resulting in different vision span in each step. In the most of the time, the attention is constrained in a local span when translating inside phrases. When emitting the fifth word "TAIRYOU", as the reordering occurs, the attention model looks globally to find the next word to translate. Analyzing the vision spans predicted by Flexible Attention in De-En task also shows similar result that the model only attends to a large span occasionally. The qualitative analysis of Flexible Attention confirms our hypothesis that attending globally in each step is redundant for machine translation. More visualizations can be found in the supplementary material.

## 6 Conclusion

In this paper, we proposed a novel attention framework that is capable of reducing the window size of attention dynamically according to the context. In our experiments, we found the proposed model can safely reduce the window size by 56% for English-Japanese and 64% German-English task on average. For character-based models, our proposed Flexible Attention can also achieve a reduction rate of 46%.

In qualitative analysis, we found that Flexible Attention only needs to put attention on a large window occasionally, especially when long-range reordering is required. The results confirm the existence of massive redundant computation in the conventional attention mechanism. By cutting down unnecessary computation, NMT models can translate extremely long sequence efficiently or incorporate more expensive score functions.

### Acknowledgement

This work is supported by JSPS KAKENHI Grant Number 16H05872.

### References

Dzmitry Bahdanau, Kyunghyun Cho, and Yoshua Bengio. 2014. Neural machine translation by jointly learning to align and translate. *arXiv preprint arXiv:1409.0473* .

Junyoung Chung, Kyunghyun Cho, and Yoshua Bengio. 2016. A character-level decoder without explicit segmentation for neural machine translation. In *ACL*. pages 1693–1703. https://doi.org/10.18653/v1/P16-1160.

Alexandre de Brébisson and Pascal Vincent. 2016. A cheap linear attention mechanism with fast lookups and fixed-size representations. *arXiv preprint arXiv:1609.05866* .

Hideki Isozaki, Tsutomu Hirao, Kevin Duh, Katsuhito Sudoh, and Hajime Tsukada. 2010. Automatic evaluation of translation quality for distant language pairs. In *EMNLP*. pages 944–952.

G Karol, I Danihelka, A Graves, D Rezende, and D Wierstra. 2015. Draw: a recurrent neural network for image generation. In *ICML*.

Diederik Kingma and Jimmy Ba. 2014. Adam: A method for stochastic optimization. *arXiv preprint arXiv:1412.6980* .

Gurvan L'Hostis, David Grangier, and Michael Auli. 2016. Vocabulary selection strategies for neural machine translation. *arXiv preprint arXiv:1610.00072* .

Liangyou Li, Xiaofeng Wu, Santiago Cortés Vaıllo, Jun Xie, Andy Way, and Qun Liu. 2014. The dcu-ictcas mt system at wmt 2014 on german-english translation task. In *Proceedings of the Ninth Workshop on Statistical Machine Translation*. pages 136–141.

Chin-Yew Lin and Franz Josef Och. 2004. Automatic evaluation of machine translation quality using longest common subsequence and skip-bigram statistics. In *ACL*. https://doi.org/10.3115/1218955.1219032.

Thang Luong, Hieu Pham, and D. Christopher Manning. 2015a. Effective approaches to attention-based neural machine translation. In *EMNLP*. pages 1412–1421. https://doi.org/10.18653/v1/D15-1166.

Thang Luong, Ilya Sutskever, Quoc Le, Oriol Vinyals, and Wojciech Zaremba. 2015b. Addressing the rare word problem in neural machine translation. In *ACL*. pages 11–19.

Toshiaki Nakazawa, Manabu Yaguchi, Kiyotaka Uchimoto, Masao Utiyama, Eiichiro Sumita, Sadao Kurohashi, and Hitoshi Isahara. 2016. Aspec: Asian scientific paper excerpt corpus. In *Proceedings of the Ninth International Conference on Language Resources and Evaluation (LREC 2016)*. pages 2204–2208.

Graham Neubig, Yosuke Nakata, and Shinsuke Mori. 2011. Pointwise prediction for robust, adaptable japanese morphological analysis. In *ACL*. pages 529–533.

Rico Sennrich, Barry Haddow, and Alexandra Birch. 2016. Neural machine translation of rare words with subword units. In *ACL*. pages 1715–1725. https://doi.org/10.18653/v1/P16-1162.

Richard Socher, Danqi Chen, Christopher D Manning, and Andrew Ng. 2013. Reasoning with neural tensor networks for knowledge base completion. In *NIPS*, pages 926–934.

Ilya Sutskever, Oriol Vinyals, and Quoc VV Le. 2014. Sequence to sequence learning with neural networks. In *NIPS*. pages 3104–3112.

Yonghui Wu, Mike Schuster, Zhifeng Chen, Quoc V Le, Mohammad Norouzi, Wolfgang Macherey, Maxim Krikun, Yuan Cao, Qin Gao, Klaus Macherey, et al. 2016. Google's neural machine translation system: Bridging the gap between human and machine translation. *arXiv preprint arXiv:1609.08144* .

Zichao Yang, Zhiting Hu, Yuntian Deng, Chris Dyer, and Alex Smola. 2016. Neural machine translation with recurrent attention modeling. *arXiv preprint arXiv:1607.05108* .

## A  Supplemental Material

In order to give a better intuition for the conclusion in 5.6, we show a visionization of the vision spans our proposed Flexible Attention predicted on the De-En development corpus. The NMT model can translate well without attending to all positions in each step. In contrast the conventional attention models, Flexible Attention only attends to a large window occasionally.

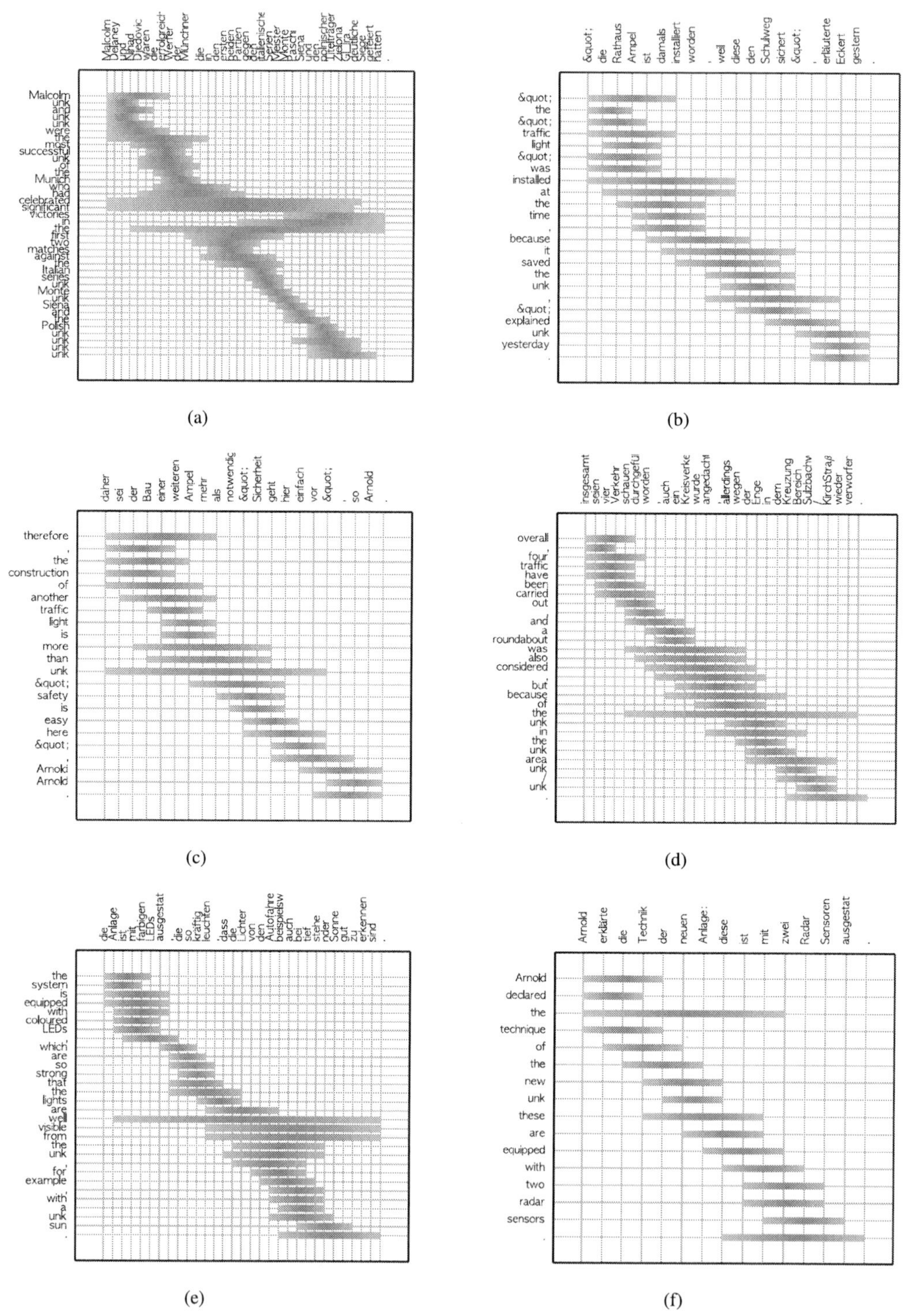

Figure 4: A visionization of the vision spans predicted by Flexible Attention for six random long sentences in the De-En development corpus

# Analyzing Neural MT Search and Model Performance


**Jan Niehues, Eunah Cho, Thanh-Le Ha, Alex Waibel**
Institute for Anthropomatics and Robotics
Karlsruhe Institute of Technology, Germany
`{jan.niehues,eunah.cho,thanh-le.ha,alex.waibel}@kit.edu`



## Abstract

In this paper, we offer an in-depth analysis about the modeling and search performance. We address the question if a more complex search algorithm is necessary. Furthermore, we investigate the question if more complex models which might only be applicable during rescoring are promising.

By separating the search space and the modeling using $n$-best list reranking, we analyze the influence of both parts of an NMT system independently. By comparing differently performing NMT systems, we show that the better translation is already in the search space of the translation systems with less performance. This results indicate that the current search algorithms are sufficient for the NMT systems. Furthermore, we could show that even a relatively small $n$-best list of 50 hypotheses already contain notably better translations.


## 1   Introduction

Recent advances in NMT systems (Bahdanau et al., 2014; Cho et al., 2014) have shown impressive results in improving machine translation tasks. Not only it performed greatly in recent machine translation campaigns (Cettolo et al., 2015; Bojar et al., 2016) measured in BLEU (Papineni et al., 2002), it is considered to be able to generate sentences with better fluency.

Despite the successful results in translation performance, however, the optimality of the search algorithm in NMT has been left under-explored. In this work, we analyze the influence of search and modeling of an NMT system by evaluating them

separately. We aim to demonstrate whether further research on the model development is more promising or the one on the search algorithm would be more beneficial.

We attempt to simulate this by $n$-best rescoring using different models. For this, $n$-best lists are rescored by different models including the one which generated them. Additionally we build a configuration with all $n$-best lists joined, in order to see whether rescoring this joined $n$-best list using the same model would bring a performance boost.

## 2   Related Work

There has been a number of works devoted to combine different systems from the same or different machine translation (MT) paradigms using $n$-best lists of hypotheses (Matusov et al., 2006; Heafield et al., 2009; Macherey and Och, 2007). The hypotheses are aligned, combined and scored by a model to produce the best candidate according to a metric. There was a thorough analysis on how the size of $n$, the diversity of the outputs from different systems and performance of individual systems can affect the final translation of the system combination. Hildebrand and Vogel (2008) examine the feature impact and the $n$-best list size of such a combination of phrase-based, hierarchical and example-based systems. Gimpel et al. (2013) show how diversity of the outputs and the size of the $n$-best lists determine the performance of the combined system.

Costa-Jussà et al. (2007) analyze the impact of the beam size used in statistical machine translation (SMT) systems. Wisniewski and Yvon (2013) conduct an in-depth analysis over several types of errors. Based on their proposal to effectively calculate oracle BLEU score for an SMT system, they can separate the errors due to the restriction of the




*Proceedings of the First Workshop on Neural Machine Translation*, pages 11–17,
Vancouver, Canada, August 4, 2017. ©2017 Association for Computational Linguistics

search space (search error) from the errors due to models not good enough to cover the best translation (model error). Although this work is the closest to our work in terms of analysis methods, our work differs from theirs by addressing the issue focused on the NMT systems.

In Neubig et al. (2015), the size of the $n$-best list produced by a phrase-based SMT and rescored by an NMT is taken into account for an error investigation. The work also shows which types of errors from the phrase-based system can be corrected or improved after NMT rescoring. To the best of our knowledge, our work is the first to examine the impact of search and model performance in pure NMT systems.

## 2.1 Neural Machine Translation

Neural machine translation, whilst considered to be in the same direction with phrase-based SMT from a statistical perspective, is actually separable from traditional SMT in terms of how it models the representation of source and target sentences as well as the translation relationship between them. In this section, we describe the general architecture of a NMT system in order to understand the needs and importance of such an analysis. The NMT architecture described here is similar to the attention-based NMT from Bahdanau et al. (2014).

An attentional NMT system consists of an encoder representing a source sentence and an attention-aware decoder that produces the translated sentence.

The encoder which is comprised of bidirectional recurrent layers reads words from the source sentence and encodes them into annotation vectors. Each annotation vector contains the information of the source sentence related to the corresponding word from both forward and backward directions.

A single layer featuring attention mechanism allows the decoder to decide which source words should take part in the prediction process of the current target word. Basically, attention layer examines a context vector of the source sentence which is weighted sum of all annotation vectors and normalized, where the weights reflect some relevance between previous target words and all the source words.

The decoder, which is also recurrent-based, recursively generates the target candidates with their probabilities to be selected based on the context vector from the attention layer, the previous recurrent state and the embedding of the previously chosen word.

The whole network is then trained in an end-to-end fashion to learn parameters which maximizes the likelihood between the outputs and the references. In the testing phase, a beam search is utilized to find the most probable target sequences giving the $n$-best list from the architecture.

We could see that in NMT, therefore, the model (e.g. the ways the encoder representing a source sentence or the attentional layer modeling attention mechanism) and the search algorithm are one of the most important aspects to be analyzed.

## 3 Search and Model Performance

In this analysis we evaluate the search and modeling performance of NMT. In order to evaluate them individually, we need to separate the modeling errors and the search errors of the system. While the search in phrase-based MT was relatively complex, the search algorithm in NMT is relatively straightforward. In state-of-the-art system, a beam search algorithm is used with a small beam between $10 - 50$.

The goal of this work is to establish whether improvements on the NMT model itself is more promising or the ones on the search algorithm. If there are many search errors due to the pruning during decoding, a better search algorithm would be promising. In contrast, if there are relatively few search errors, further research on the model is more promising.

### 3.1 Analysis Setup

A straightforward way would be to evaluate all possible hypotheses. In this case we do not have any search error and can directly measure the modeling errors. However this cannot be performed efficiently since the number of all possible hypotheses is very large. Therefore, we analyzed the performance of two or several systems with different performances.

In the experiments, for example, we have systems $A$ and $B$ where the translation performance of $A$ is better than the one of $B$. Then we approximated the search space of $A$ and $B$ by their $n$-best lists and evaluated the performance of each system in the search space of $A$ by scoring the $n$-best list with the model and selecting the hypothesis with

Figure 1: Search space analysis

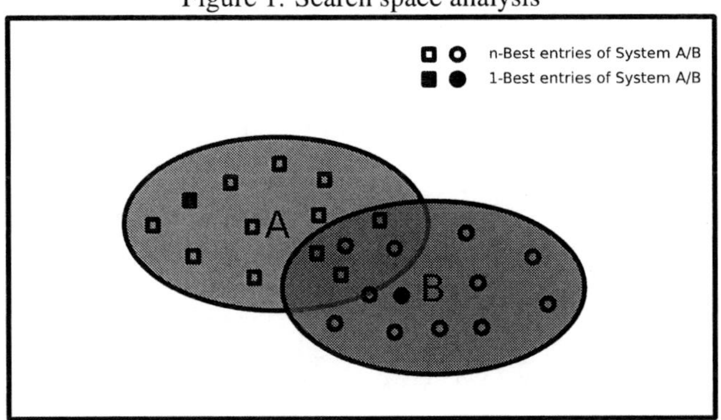


the highest probability. Figure 1 shows the search spaces of system $A$ and $B$, approximated by their $n$-best hypotheses. Their 1-best entries are also marked accordingly.

The question we address is why the system $B$ did select its best hypothesis ● and did not select the better-performant hypothesis ■. One reason might be that ■ is not in the system B's search space and therefore the system could not find it. The other reason might be that system $B$ prefers ● over ■. In this case, we need to improve the modelling.

If the performance of model $B$ on the $n$-best list of $A$ is better than the initial score of $B$, it suggests that the model $B$ is able to select a better hypothesis and therefore the search is not optimal. On the other hand, if the performance is similar, it means that $B$ is not able to select a better hypothesis, even though there are better ones according to the evaluation metric.

In the experiments, we used two different ways of constructing the models $A$ and $B$. In a first series of experiments, we used the single best system as well as ensemble systems. In a second series, we used systems using different ways to generate the translations. Details of the systems will be given in the Section 4.

## 4 System Description

Our German↔English NMT systems are built using an encoder-decoder framework with attention mechanism, nematus.[1] Byte pair encoding (BPE) is used in order to generate sub-word units (Sennrich et al., 2015). Long sentences whose sentence length exceeds 50 words are ex-

empted from the training. We use minibatch size 80 and sentences are shuffled within every minibatch. Word embedding of size 500 is applied, with hidden layers of size 1024. Dropout is applied at every layer with the probability 0.2 in the embedding and hidden layers and 0.1 in the input and output layers. Our models are trained with Adadelta (Zeiler, 2012) and the gradient norm is clipped to 1.0. For the single models, we apply the early stopping based on the validation score.

The baseline system is trained on the WMT parallel data, namely EPPS, NC, CommonCrawl and TED corpus. As validation data we used the newstest13 set from IWSLT evaluation campaign. Therefore, this data is from TED talks. Test is applied on two domains. First domain is TED talks, same as the optimization set. We use newstest14 for this testing. Another domain is telephone conversation and we used MSLT (Christian Federmann, 2016) for testing. Since no exact genre-matching development data is published for the evaluation campaign (Cettolo et al., 2015), we used the TED-optimized system for the MSLT testing. For each experiment, we also offer oracle BLEU scores on the $n$-best lists, calculated using multeval (Clark et al., 2011).

### 4.1 Configurations

We tried different system configurations to generate and rescore the $n$-best lists. By using 40K operations of BPE we had *SmallVoc* configuration, and with 80K *BigVoc* configuration. In *SmallVoc.rev*, target sentence are generated in the reversed order. In *SmallVoc.mix*, target side corpus is joined with the source side corpus to form a mixed input as described in Cho et al. (2016). We build an NMT system which takes pre-translation

---

[1] https://github.com/rsennrich/nematus

from a PBMT system following the work in Niehues et al. (2016), which will be referred as *PrePBMT*. A configuration using more monolingual data for this training is called *PrePBMT.large*. In *Union*, we use the joined $n$-best lists from different systems.

### 4.2 $n$-best list

All $n$-best lists are generated for $n = 50$ from a standard beam search. The size of $n$-best lists are limited due to time and computational limitation. In our preliminary experiments where we increased $n$-best list from 1 to 50, it did not significantly change the performance of one model. Therefore, in this work, we approximate the 50-best lists our search space and conducted the analysis. By doing so, we also aim to give a practical analysis on a model vs. search performance comparison in NMT and useful guidelines from it.

## 5 Analysis on the Results

In this section, we discuss the experimental results and detailed analysis. In the first part, we discuss the results of the experiments on the baseline systems. In the second part, we combine NMT systems that use different text representations.

### 5.1 NMT Baseline Systems

In this section, we analyze the performance of baseline systems. It largely breaks down to two tasks: TED and MSLT translation.

#### 5.1.1 TED translation

Table 1 shows the baseline system performance on the TED translation task, from German to English. The table is showing translation performance of reranking each $n$-best list using different models.

| Model<br>$n$-best | Single | Ensemble | Oracle |
|---|---|---|---|
| Single | 31.96 | 32.37 | 41.81 |
| Ensemble | 32.09 | 32.41 | 42.31 |
| Union | 31.95 | 32.39 | 44.55 |

Table 1: Baseline: TED German→English

For the *Single* system, we took the best-performant *BigVoc* system. The *Ensemble* system is then generated by combining several training steps of the single system training. The *Union* $n$-best list is the joined $n$-best list of all the individual systems used in the ensemble. For building a *Ensemble* system, we combine different models from several time steps of *Single* training. Then in the softmax operation, normalized probabilities of each word are considered. As mentioned earlier, we also offer the oracle BLEU scores given each $n$-best list.

**Model performance** As shown in the table, we can improve the translation performance by 0.5 BLEU point by using the *Ensemble* system to rescore $n$-best list generated by the same system, compared to the same case for *Single* system. The main contribution for this improvement seems to be the better modeling. When we use the *Single* model to rescore the *Ensemble* or *Union* $n$-best list, we get mainly the same performance. Thus, the reason for the relatively lower performance of the *Single* system is considered to be that it does not model the translation probabilities better, not because it does not find better translations. The oracle scores indicate the similar trend. When the $n$-best list is large (*Union* setup), we have better translations in the $n$-best list. However, these hypotheses were not selected by either of the models.

**Search performance** The numbers in Table 1 suggests that the search is well-performant in NMT. For example, when we use the *Ensemble* model to rescore the *Single* $n$-best list, the translation performance reaches 32.37 BLEU points. At the same time, when we use the same model to rescore the *Ensemble* $n$-best list, we achieve a similar performance.

#### 5.1.2 MSLT translation

The performance on the single system on the MSLT task (Christian Federmann, 2016) is shown in Table 2.

| Model<br>$n$-best | Single | Ensemble | Oracle |
|---|---|---|---|
| Single | 34.63 | 38.35 | 53.85 |
| Ensemble | 35.94 | 38.80 | 56.46 |

Table 2: Baseline: MSLT German→English

In this task, rescoring *Single* $n$-best list using the same model itself performs around 4 BLEU worse than rescoring *Ensemble* $n$-best list using the *Ensemble* model. Also, we can observe that the *Single* model performs better when using the $n$-best list of the *Ensemble* model.

We find two explanations for this improvement. A) The *Ensemble* $n$-best list contains better-performing hypotheses that the *Single* model did not find during the search. Or alternatively, B) the *Ensemble* $n$-best list does not contain the hypotheses that are good according to the *Single* model but not according to the evaluation metric. In this case, the model would select different hypotheses.

In order to locate search error, we evaluated and compared the model score of hypothesis chosen from different $n$-best lists. Only in 2.5% of the chosen hypotheses, the score of the hypothesis selected from the *Ensemble* $n$-best list is higher than the one from the *Single* $n$-best list. Thus, we have a search error only in these cases.

In contrast, in 90.7% of the sentences, the score from the *Single* $n$-best list is higher. The main reason for the improvement, therefore, is not considered to be better search. Rather, the search space by the *Ensemble* system does not contain the worse-performing translations which are highly ranked by the *Single* system.

The $n$-best lists of the *Single* model contains well-performing translations. For example, the performance achieved when using the *Ensemble* model to rescore the *Single* $n$-best list is almost similar to the one achieved when applying the same model on the *Ensemble* $n$-best list. This performance is nearly 4 BLEU points better than rescoring the same $n$-best list using the *Single* model.

While the performance of the *Ensemble* model on both $n$-best lists is similar, interestingly, the oracle score of the *Ensemble* $n$-best list is clearly higher. Therefore, the models seem not able to select better translations in the *Ensemble* $n$-best list compared to the *Single* $n$-best list.

### 5.2 NMT Text Representation Systems

As a next line of experiment, we combine NMT systems that use different text representations.

#### 5.2.1 TED translation

Table 3 lists the systems used in the experiment and their performance on the TED task.

We can observe that the results of *Union* rescored by each model is similar to the performance of the model's $n$-best list rescoring, as marked in bold letters in each column. Considering that the *Union* $n$-best list is considerably larger, it seems again that the model can find the best hypothesis according to the model.

In contrast, if we use all models (*All*) by using sum of log probabilities of all models to rescore the $n$-best lists, we achieve similar performance for all $n$-best lists. Thus, it seems that all 50-best lists contain already very good hypotheses. Only the $n$-best list of the *PrePBMT* system seems to contain relatively worse options. This is also shown by the oracle scores. One reason could be that the pre-translation by the PBMT system is guiding the search and therefore the $n$-best list contains relatively limited variety.

In addition, we observe that the performance of each model on its own $n$-best list is considerably worse than the model rescoring other $n$-best lists. This can be explained by the following phenomena: some translations of a system $A$ are highly-ranked by the model itself, but not by the others. Therefore, they are selected by the system $A$ but not in the $n$-best lists of the other systems. If they are in the $n$-best list, e.g. in the $n$-best lists of the system $A$ and in the *Union*, they will be selected only when using the system $A$, leading to worse performance in BLEU. In contrast, if we use different $n$-best lists, the translation performance is better.

**English→German**  In addition, we extend this experiment to another language direction. Table 4 shows the results when the same experiment is applied to En-De TED task.

Here the same phenomena is observed. Again, the *Union* $n$-best list does not improve the translation quality. Nonetheless, the oracle score is significantly higher indicating that the model finds the better hypotheses. Furthermore, the $n$-best lists already contain better hypotheses which can be chosen using better models, i.g. the combination of all models.

#### 5.2.2 MSLT translation

Table 5 shows the similar results when the same experiments are applied to the MSLT task. The *Union* configuration performs similar to rescoring using the same model, while performing considerably worse than the case where the same $n$-best list rescored by other models.

## 6 Conclusion

Our experiments on two language pairs and two different tasks showed that there are only few search errors in the state-of-the-art NMT systems. Even when better hypotheses are added in the $n$-best list, the models do not select a different hypothesis. Thus, the search algorithms seem to be

| Model<br>$n$-best list | SmallVoc | SmallVoc.rev | BigVoc | PrePBMT | All | Oracle |
|---|---|---|---|---|---|---|
| SmallVoc | **31.74** | 32.17 | 32.62 | 32.55 | 33.03 | 41.82 |
| SmallVoc.rev | 32.24 | **31.28** | 32.58 | 32.06 | 32.93 | 40.97 |
| BigVoc | 32.57 | 32.50 | **32.41** | 32.63 | 33.26 | 42.31 |
| PrePBMT | 32.19 | 31.97 | 32.53 | **31.41** | 32.65 | 40.67 |
| Union | **31.83** | **31.27** | **32.42** | **31.39** | 33.24 | 46.58 |

Table 3: Text representation systems: TED German→English

| Model<br>$n$-best list | SmallVoc.mix | BigVoc | PrePBMT | PrePBMT.large | All | Oracle |
|---|---|---|---|---|---|---|
| SmallVoc.mix | **26.19** | 27.09 | 26.93 | 27.03 | 27.12 | 33.71 |
| BigVoc | 26.97 | **27.28** | 27.26 | 27.12 | 27.48 | 34.16 |
| PrePBMT | 26.96 | 27.00 | **26.44** | 27.15 | 27.14 | 32.95 |
| PrePBMT.large | 27.25 | 27.47 | 26.85 | **27.03** | 27.41 | 33.78 |
| Union | **26.25** | **27.28** | **26.44** | **27.03** | 27.76 | 38.95 |

Table 4: Text representation systems: TED English→German

sufficient.

Furthermore, we showed that a relatively small $n$-best list of 50 entries already contains notably better translation hypotheses. This result indicates that improving rescoring models are promising for performance boost. In this work, we showed that it is often sufficient to use a model in rescoring only. This finding also motivates the development of models which are challenging to use directly during the decoding, such as bi-directional decoders.

## Acknowledgments

The project leading to this application has received funding from the European Union's Horizon 2020 research and innovation programme under grant agreement n° 645452. The research by Thanh-Le Ha was supported by Ministry of Science, Research and the Arts Baden-Württemberg. This work was supported by the Carl-Zeiss-Stiftung.

## References

Dzmitry Bahdanau, Kyunghyun Cho, and Yoshua Bengio. 2014. Neural Machine Translation by Jointly Learning to Align and Translate. *CoRR* abs/1409.0473. http://arxiv.org/abs/1409.0473.

Ondrej Bojar, Rajen Chatterjee, Christian Federmann, Barry Haddow, Philipp Koehn, Johannes Leveling, Christof Monz, Pavel Pecina, Matt Post, Herve Saint-Amand, et al. 2016. Findings of the 2016 Conference on Machine Translation (WMT16). In *Proceedings of the First Conference on Machine Translation (WMT16)*. Association for Computational Linguistics, Berlin, Germany, pages 12–58.

M Cettolo, J Niehues, S Stüker, L Bentivogli, and M Federico. 2015. The IWSLT 2016 Evaluation Campaign. In *Proceedings of the 13th International Workshop on Spoken Language Translation (IWSLT 2015)*. Seattle, US.

Eunah Cho, Jan Niehues, Thanh-Le Le, Matthias Sperber, Mohammed Mediani, and Alex Waibel. 2016. Adaptation and combination of nmt systems: The kit translation systems for iwslt 2016. In *IWSLT*. Seattle, WA, USA.

Kyunghyun Cho, Bart Van Merriënboer, Caglar Gulcehre, Dzmitry Bahdanau, Fethi Bougares, Holger Schwenk, and Yoshua Bengio. 2014. Learning phrase representations using rnn encoder-decoder for statistical machine translation. In *Proceedings of the 2014 Conference on Empirical Methods in Natural Language Processing (EMNLP 2014)*. Doha, Qatar.

William D. Lewis Christian Federmann. 2016. Microsoft speech language translation (mslt) corpus: The iwslt 2016 release for english, french and german. In *IWSLT*. Seattle, WA, USA.

Jonathan H. Clark, Chris Dyer, Alon Lavie, and Noah A. Smith. 2011. Better hypothesis testing for statistical machine translation: Controlling for optimizer instability. In *Proceedings of the 49th Annual Meeting of the Association for Computational Linguistics: Human Language Technologies: Short Papers - Volume 2*. Association for Computational Linguistics, Stroudsburg, PA, USA, HLT '11, pages 176–181. http://dl.acm.org/citation.cfm?id=2002736.2002774.

| Model<br>$n$-best list | SmallVoc | SmallVoc.rev | BigVoc | PrePBMT | All | Oracle |
|---|---|---|---|---|---|---|
| SmallVoc | **37.90** | 39.50 | 39.35 | 39.05 | 40.30 | 56.41 |
| SmallVoc.rev | 39.74 | **38.72** | 39.92 | 39.94 | 40.80 | 56.82 |
| BigVoc | 38.73 | 39.61 | **38.80** | 39.51 | 40.25 | 56.46 |
| PrePBMT | 38.91 | 39.68 | 39.36 | **38.33** | 40.24 | 54.44 |
| Union | **37.92** | **38.65** | **38.81** | **38.33** | 40.66 | 63.09 |

Table 5: Text representation systems: MSLT German→English


Marta R Costa-Jussà, Josep M Crego, David Vilar, José AR Fonollosa, José B Mariño, and Hermann Ney. 2007. Analysis and System Combination of Phrase-and N-gram-based Statistical Machine Translation Systems. In *The Conference of the North American Chapter of the Association for Computational Linguistics (NAACLT'07)*. Association for Computational Linguistics, Rochester, NY, USA, pages 137–140.

Kevin Gimpel, Dhruv Batra, Chris Dyer, and Gregory Shakhnarovich. 2013. A Systematic Exploration of Diversity in Machine Translation. In *Proceedings of the 2013 Conference on Empirical Methods in Natural Language Processing (EMNLP'13)*. Seattle, WA, USA.

Kenneth Heafield, Greg Hanneman, and Alon Lavie. 2009. Machine translation system combination with flexible word ordering. In *Proceedings of the Fourth Workshop on Statistical Machine Translation (WMT'09)*. Association for Computational Linguistics, Athens, Greece, pages 56–60.

Almut Silja Hildebrand and Stephan Vogel. 2008. Combination of Machine Translation Systems via Hypothesis Selection from Combined N-Best Lists. In *Proceedings of the Eighth Conference of the Association for Machine Translation in the Americas (AMTA'08)*. Hawaii, USA, pages 254–261.

Wolfgang Macherey and Franz J Och. 2007. An empirical study on computing consensus translations from multiple machine translation systems .

Evgeny Matusov, Nicola Ueffing, and Hermann Ney. 2006. Computing Consensus Translation for Multiple Machine Translation Systems Using Enhanced Hypothesis Alignment. In *Proceedings of the 11th Conference of the European Chapter of Association for Computational Linguistics (EACL 2006)*. Association for Computational Linguistics, Trento, Italy, pages 56–60.

Graham Neubig, Makoto Morishita, and Satoshi Nakamura. 2015. Neural Reranking Improves Subjective Quality of Machine Translation: NAIST at WAT2015. In *Proceedings of the 2nd Workshop on Asian Translation (WAT'15)*. Kyoto, Japan.

Jan Niehues, Eunah Cho, Thanh-Le Ha, and Alex Waibel. 2016. Pre-translation for neural machine translation. In *the 26th International Conference on Computational Linguistics (Coling 2016)*.

Kishore Papineni, Salim Roukos, Todd Ward, and Wei-Jing Zhu. 2002. Bleu: A method for automatic evaluation of machine translation. In *Proceedings of the 40th Annual Meeting on Association for Computational Linguistics (ACL 2002)*. Association for Computational Linguistics, Philadelphia, Pennsylvania, USA, pages 311–318.

Rico Sennrich, Barry Haddow, and Alexandra Birch. 2015. Neural machine translation of rare words with subword units. In *Proceedings of the 54th Annual Meeting of the Association for Computational Linguistics*. Berlin, Germany.

Guillaume Wisniewski and François Yvon. 2013. Oracle Decoding as a New Way to Analyze Phrase-based Machine Translation. *Machine Translation* 27(2):115–138.

Matthew D Zeiler. 2012. Adadelta: an adaptive learning rate method. In *CoRR*.

# Stronger Baselines for Trustable Results in Neural Machine Translation


**Michael Denkowski**
Amazon.com, Inc.
`mdenkows@amazon.com`

**Graham Neubig**
Carnegie Mellon University
`gneubig@cs.cmu.edu`



## Abstract

Interest in neural machine translation has grown rapidly as its effectiveness has been demonstrated across language and data scenarios. New research regularly introduces architectural and algorithmic improvements that lead to significant gains over "vanilla" NMT implementations. However, these new techniques are rarely evaluated in the context of previously published techniques, specifically those that are widely used in state-of-the-art production and shared-task systems. As a result, it is often difficult to determine whether improvements from research will carry over to systems deployed for real-world use. In this work, we recommend three specific methods that are relatively easy to implement and result in much stronger experimental systems. Beyond reporting significantly higher BLEU scores, we conduct an in-depth analysis of where improvements originate and what inherent weaknesses of basic NMT models are being addressed. We then compare the relative gains afforded by several other techniques proposed in the literature when starting with vanilla systems versus our stronger baselines, showing that experimental conclusions may change depending on the baseline chosen. This indicates that choosing a strong baseline is crucial for reporting reliable experimental results.


## 1 Introduction

In the relatively short time since its introduction, neural machine translation has risen to prominence in both academia and industry. Neural models have consistently shown top performance in shared evaluation tasks (Bojar et al., 2016; Cettolo et al., 2016) and are becoming the technology of choice for commercial MT service providers (Wu et al., 2016; Crego et al., 2016). New work from the research community regularly introduces model extensions and algorithms that show significant gains over baseline NMT. However, the continuous improvement of real-world translation systems has led to a substantial performance gap between the first published neural translation models and the current state of the art. When promising new techniques are only evaluated on very basic NMT systems, it can be difficult to determine how much (if any) improvement will carry over to stronger systems; is new work actually solving new problems or simply re-solving problems that have already been addressed elsewhere?

In this work, we recommend three specific techniques for strengthening NMT systems and empirically demonstrate how their use improves reliability of experimental results. We analyze in depth how these techniques change the behavior of NMT systems by addressing key weaknesses and discuss how these findings can be used to understand the effect of other types of system extensions. Our recommended techniques include: (1) a training approach using Adam with multiple restarts and learning rate annealing, (2) sub-word translation via byte pair encoding, and (3) decoding with ensembles of independently trained models.

We begin the paper content by introducing a typical NMT baseline system as our experimental starting point (§2.1). We then present and examine the effects of each recommended technique: Adam with multiple restarts and step size annealing (§3), byte pair encoding (§4), and independent model ensembling (§5). We show that combining these techniques can lead to a substantial improvement of over 5 BLEU (§6) and that results for several previously published techniques can dramati-

18


*Proceedings of the First Workshop on Neural Machine Translation*, pages 18–27,
Vancouver, Canada, August 4, 2017. ©2017 Association for Computational Linguistics

cally differ (up to being reversed) when evaluated on stronger systems (§6.2). We then conclude by summarizing our findings (§7).

## 2 Experimental Setup

### 2.1 Translation System

Our starting point for experimentation is a standard baseline neural machine translation system implemented using the Lamtram[1] and DyNet[2] toolkits (Neubig, 2015; Neubig et al., 2017). This system uses the attentional encoder-decoder architecture described by Bahdanau et al. (2015), building on work by Sutskever et al. (2014). The translation model uses a bi-directional encoder with a single LSTM layer of size 1024, multilayer perceptron attention with a layer size of 1024, and word representations of size 512. Translation models are trained until perplexity convergence on held-out data using the Adam algorithm with a maximum step size of 0.0002 (Kingma and Ba, 2015; Wu et al., 2016). Maximum training sentence length is set to 100 words. Model vocabulary is limited to the top 50K source words and 50K target words by frequency, with all others mapped to an unk token. A post-processing step replaces any unk tokens in system output by attempting a dictionary lookup[3] of the corresponding source word (highest attention score) and backing off to copying the source word directly (Luong et al., 2015). Experiments in each section evaluate this system against incremental extensions such as improved model vocabulary or training algorithm. Evaluation is conducted by average BLEU score over multiple independent training runs (Papineni et al., 2002; Clark et al., 2011).

### 2.2 Data Sets

We evaluate systems on a selection of public data sets covering a range of data sizes, language directions, and morphological complexities. These sets, described in Table 1, are drawn from shared translation tasks at the 2016 ACL Conference on Machine Translation (WMT16)[4] and the 2016 International Workshop on Spoken Language Translation (IWSLT16)[5].

---



| Scenario | Size (sent) | Sources |
|---|---|---|
| WMT German-English | 4,562,102 | Europarl, Common Crawl, news commentary |
| WMT English-Finnish | 2,079,842 | Europarl, Wikipedia titles |
| WMT Romanian-English | 612,422 | Europarl, SETimes |
| IWSLT English-French | 220,400 | TED talks |
| IWSLT Czech-English | 114,390 | TED talks |

| Scenario | Validation (Dev) Set | Test Set |
|---|---|---|
| DE-EN | News test 2015 | News test 2016 |
| EN-FI | News test 2015 | News test 2016 |
| RO-EN | News dev 2016 | News test 2016 |
| EN-FR | TED test 2013+2014 | TED test 2015+2016 |
| CS-EN | TED test 2012+2013 | TED test 2015+2016 |

Table 1: Top: parallel training data available for all scenarios. Bottom: validation and test sets.

## 3 Training Algorithms

### 3.1 Background

The first neural translation models were optimized with stochastic gradient descent (Sutskever et al., 2014). After training for several epochs with a fixed learning rate, the rate is halved at prespecified intervals. This widely used rate "annealing" technique takes large steps to move parameters from their initial point to a promising part of the search space followed by increasingly smaller steps to explore that part of the space for a good local optimum. While effective, this approach can be time consuming and relies on hand-crafted learning schedules that may not generalize to different models and data sets.

To eliminate the need for schedules, subsequent NMT work trained models using the Adadelta algorithm, which automatically and continuously adapts learning rates for individual parameters during training (Zeiler, 2012). Model performance is reported to be equivalent to SGD with annealing, though training still takes a considerable amount of time (Bahdanau et al., 2015; Sennrich et al., 2016b). More recent work seeks to accelerate training with the Adam algorithm, which applies momentum on a per-parameter basis and automatically adapts step size subject to a user-specified maximum (Kingma and Ba, 2015). While this can lead to much faster convergence, the resulting models are shown to slightly underperform compared to annealing SGD (Wu et al., 2016). However, Adam's speed and reputation

---

[1] https://github.com/neubig/lamtram
[2] https://github.com/clab/dynet
[3] Translation dictionaries are learned from the system's training data using fast_align (Dyer et al., 2013).
[4] http://statmt.org/wmt16 (Bojar et al., 2016)
[5] https://workshop2016.iwslt.org, https://wit3.fbk.eu (Cettolo et al., 2012)

of generally being "good enough" have made it a popular choice for researchers and NMT toolkit authors[6] (Arthur et al., 2016; Lee et al., 2016; Britz et al., 2017; Sennrich et al., 2017).

While differences in automatic metric scores between SGD and Adam-trained systems may be relatively small, they raise the more general question of training effectiveness. In the following section, we explore the relative quality of the optima found by these training algorithms.

### 3.2 Results and Analysis

To compare the behavior of SGD and Adam, we conduct training experiments with all data sets listed in §2.2. For each set, we train instances of the baseline model described in §2.1 with both optimizers using empirically effective initial settings.[7] In the only departure from the described baseline, we use a byte-pair encoded vocabulary with 32K merge operations in place of a limited full-word vocabulary, leading to faster training and higher metric scores (see experiments in §4).

For SGD, we begin with a learning rate of 0.5 and train the model to convergence as measured by dev set perplexity. We then halve the learning rate and restart training from the best previous point. This continues until training has been run a total of 5 times. The choice of training to convergence is made both to avoid the need for hand-crafted learning schedules and to give the optimizers a better chance to find good neighborhoods to explore. For Adam, we use a learning rate (maximum step size) of 0.0002. While Adam's use of momentum can be considered a form of "self-annealing", we also evaluate the novel extension of explicitly annealing the maximum step size by applying the same halving and restarting process used for SGD. It is important to note that while restarting SGD has no effect beyond changing the learning rate, restarting Adam causes the optimizer to "forget" the per-parameter learning rates and start fresh.

For all training, we use a mini-batch size of 512 words.[8] For WMT systems, we evaluate dev set perplexity every 50K training sentences for the first training run and every 25K sentences for subsequent runs. For IWSLT systems, we evaluate every 25K sentences and then every 6,250 sentences. Training stops when no improvement in perplexity has been seen in 20 evaluations. For each experimental condition, we conduct 3 independent optimizer runs and report averaged metric scores. All training results are visualized in Figure 1.

Our first observation is that these experiments are largely in concert with prior work: Adam without annealing (first point) is significantly faster than SGD with annealing (last point) and often comparable or slightly worse in accuracy, with the exception of Czech-English where SGD underperforms. However, Adam with just 2 restarts and SGD-style rate annealing is actually both faster than the fully annealed SGD and obtains significantly better results in both perplexity and BLEU. We conjecture that the reason for this is twofold. First, while Adam has the ability to automatically adjust its learning rate, like SGD it still benefits from an explicit adjustment when it has begun to overfit. Second, Adam's adaptive learning rates tend to reduce to sub-optimally low values as training progresses, leading to getting stuck in a local optimum. Restarting training when reducing the learning rate helps jolt the optimizer out of this local optimum and continue to find parameters that are better globally.

## 4 Sub-Word Translation

### 4.1 Background

Unlike phrase-based approaches, neural translation models must limit source and target vocabulary size to keep computational complexity manageable. Basic models typically include the most frequent words (30K-50K) plus a single unk token to which all other words are mapped. As described in §2.1, unk words generated by the NMT system are translated in post-processing by dictionary lookup or pass-through, often with significantly degraded quality (Luong et al., 2015). Real-world NMT systems frequently sidestep this problem with sub-word translation, where models operate on a fixed number of word pieces that can be chained together to form words in an arbitrar-

---

[6] Adam is the default optimizer for the Lamtram, Nematus (https://github.com/rsennrich/nematus), and Marian toolkits (https://github.com/amunmt/marian).

[7] Learning rates of 0.5 for SGD and 0.0002 for Adam or very similar are shown to work well in NMT implementations including GNMT (Wu et al., 2016), Nematus, Marian, and OpenNMT (http://opennmt.net).

[8] For each mini-batch, sentences are added until the word count is reached. Counting words versus sentences leads to more uniformly-sized mini-batches. We choose the size of 512 based on contrastive experiments that found it to be the best balance between speed and effectiveness of updates during training.

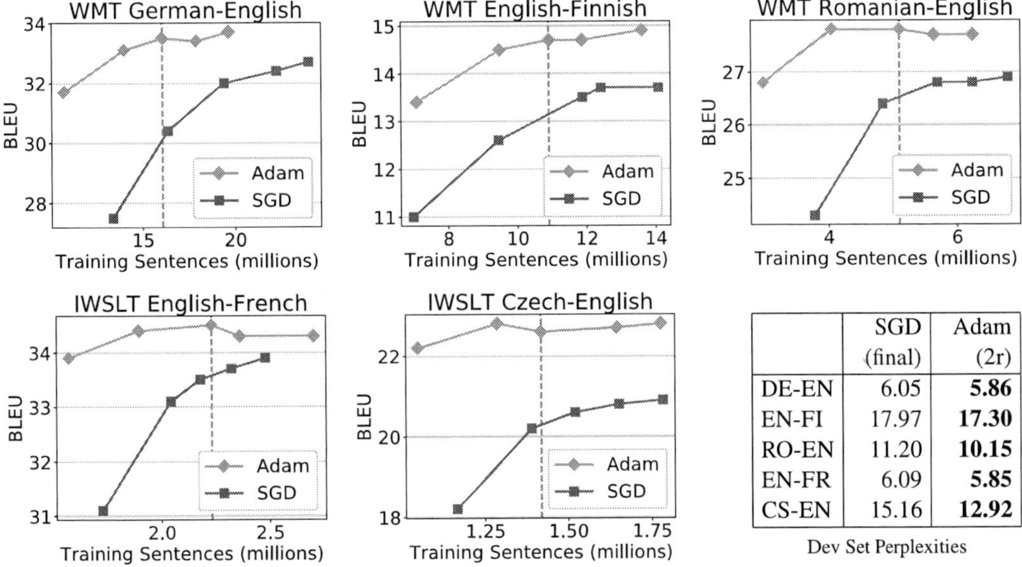

Figure 1: Results of training the NMT models with Adam and SGD using rate annealing. Each point represents training to convergence with a fixed learning rate and translating the test set. The learning rate is then halved and training resumed from the previous best point. Vertical dotted lines indicate 2 Adam restarts. The table lists dev set perplexities for the final SGD model and the 2-restart Adam model. All reported values are averaged over 3 independent training runs.

ily large vocabulary. In this section, we examine the impact of sub-words on NMT, specifically when using the technique of *byte pair encoding* (Sennrich et al., 2016b). Given the full parallel corpus (concatenation of source and target sides), BPE first splits all words into individual characters and then begins merging the most frequently adjacent pairs. Merged pairs become single units that are candidates for further merging and the process continues to build larger word pieces for a fixed number of operations. The final result is an encoded corpus where the most frequent words are single pieces and less frequent words are split into multiple, higher frequency pieces. At test time, words are split using the operations learned during training, allowing the model to translate with a nearly open vocabulary.[9] The model vocabulary size grows with and is limited by the number of merge operations. While prior work has focused on using sub-words as a method for translating

| | WMT | | | IWSLT | |
|---|---|---|---|---|---|
| | DE-EN | EN-FI | RO-EN | EN-FR | CS-EN |
| Words 50K | 31.6 | 12.6 | 27.1 | 33.6 | 21.0 |
| BPE 32K | **33.5** | **14.7** | **27.8** | 34.5 | 22.6 |
| BPE 16K | 33.1 | **14.7** | **27.8** | **34.8** | **23.0** |

Table 2: BLEU scores for training NMT models with full word and byte pair encoded vocabularies. Full word models limit vocabulary size to 50K. All models are trained with annealing Adam and scores are averaged over 3 optimizer runs.

unseen words in morphologically rich languages (Sennrich et al., 2016b) or reducing model size (Wu et al., 2016), we examine how using BPE actually leads to broad improvement by addressing inherent weaknesses of word-level NMT.

## 4.2 Results and Analysis

We measure the effects of byte pair encoding by training full-word and BPE systems for all data sets as described in §2.1 with the incremental improvement of using Adam with rate annealing (§3). As Wu et al. (2016) show different levels of effectiveness for different sub-word vocabulary sizes, we evaluate running BPE with 16K and 32K

---

[9]It is possible that certain intermediate word pieces will not appear in the encoded training data (and thus the model's vocabulary) if all occurrences are merged into larger units. If these pieces appear in test data and are not merged, they will be true OOVs for the model. For this reason, we map singleton word pieces in the training data to unk so the model has some ability to handle these cases (dictionary lookup or pass-through).

merge operations. As shown in Table 2, sub-word systems outperform full-word systems across the board, despite having fewer total parameters. Systems built on larger data generally benefit from larger vocabularies while smaller systems perform better with smaller vocabularies. Based on these results, we recommend 32K as a generally effective vocabulary size and 16K as a contrastive condition when building systems on less than 1 million parallel sentences.

To understand the origin of these improvements, we divide the words in each test set into classes based on how the full-word and BPE models handle them and report the unigram F-1 score for each model on each class. We also plot the full-word and BPE vocabularies for context. As shown in Figure 2, performance is comparable for the most frequent words that both models represent as single units. The identical shapes on the leftmost part of each vocabulary plot indicate that the two systems have the same number of training instances from which to learn translations. For words that are split in the BPE model, performance is tied to data sparsity. With larger data, performance is comparable as both models have enough training instances to learn reliable statistics; with smaller data or morphologically rich languages such as Finnish, significant gains can be realized by modeling multiple higher-frequency sub-words in place of a single lower-frequency word. This can be seen as effectively moving to the left in the vocabulary plot where translations are more reliable. In the next category of words beyond the 50K cutoff, the BPE system's ability to actually model rare words leads to consistent improvement over the full-word system's reliance on dictionary substitution.

The final two categories evaluate handling of true out-of-vocabulary items. For OOVs that should be translated, the full-word system will always score zero, lacking any mechanism for producing words not in its vocabulary or dictionary. The more interesting result is in the relatively low scores for OOVs that should simply be copied from source to target. While phrase-based systems can reliably pass OOVs through 1:1, full-word neural systems must generate unk tokens and correctly map them to source words using attention scores. Differences in source and target true vocabulary sizes and frequency distributions often lead to different numbers of unk to-kens in source and target sentences, resulting in models that are prone to over or under-generating unks at test time. BPE systems address these weaknesses, although their performance is not always intuitive. While some OOVs are successfully translated using word pieces, overall scores are still quite low, indicating only limited success for the notion of open vocabulary translation often associated with sub-word NMT. However, the ability to learn when to self-translate sub-words[10] leads to significant gains in pass-through accuracy.

In summary, our analysis indicates that while BPE does lead to smaller, faster models, it also significantly improves translation quality. Rather than being limited to only rare and unseen words, modeling higher-frequency sub-words in place of lower-frequency full words can lead to significant improvement across the board. The specific improvement in pass-through OOV handling can be particularly helpful for handling named entities and open-class items such as numbers and URLs without additional dedicated techniques.

## 5  Ensembles and Model Diversity

The final technique we explore is the combination of multiple translation models into a single, more powerful *ensemble* by averaging their predictions at the word level. The idea of ensemble averaging is well understood and widely used across machine learning fields and work from the earliest encoder-decoder papers to the most recent system descriptions reports dramatic improvements in BLEU scores for model ensembles (Sutskever et al., 2014; Sennrich et al., 2016a). While this technique is conceptually simple, it requires training and decoding with multiple translation models, often at significant resource costs. However, these costs are either mitigated or justified when building real-world systems or evaluating techniques that should be applicable to those systems. Decoding costs can be reduced by using *knowledge distillation* techniques to train a single, compact model to replicate the output of an ensemble (Hinton et al., 2015; Kuncoro et al., 2016; Kim and Rush, 2016). Researchers can skip this time-consuming step, evaluating the ensemble directly, while real-world system engineers can rely on it to make deployment of ensembles practical. To re-

---

[10]Learning a single set of BPE operations by concatenating the source and target training data ensures that the same word will always be segmented in the same way whether it appears on the source or target side.

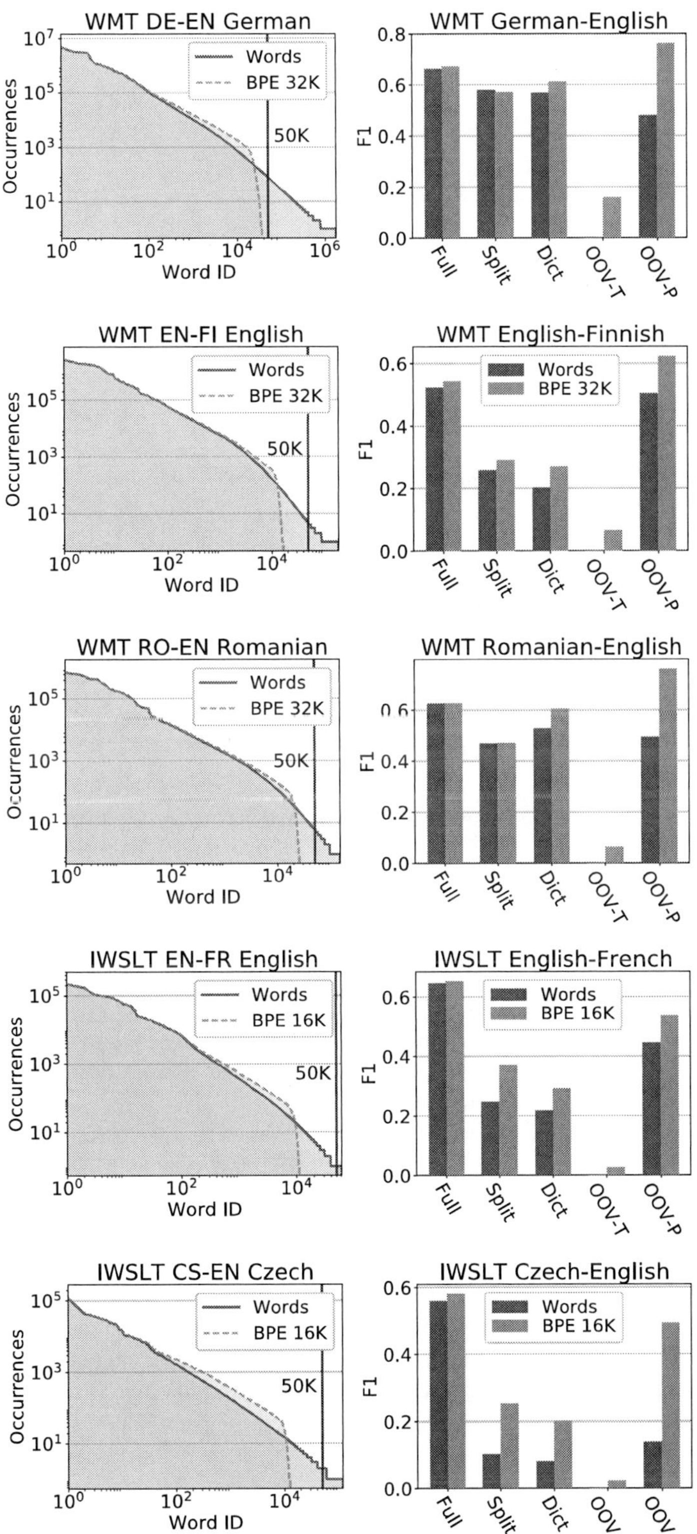

Figure 2: Effects of using sub-word units on model vocabulary and translation accuracy for specific types of words.

**Left figures:** Source vocabulary visualizations for NMT training data using full words and byte-pair encoded tokens. The number of merge operations is set to either 32K or 16K, chosen by best BLEU score. BPE reduces vocabulary size by 1-2 orders of magnitude and allows models to cover the entire training corpus. Full-word systems for all scenarios use a much larger vocabulary size of 50K (labeled horizontal line) that leaves much of the total vocabulary uncovered.

**Right figures:** Class-wise test set unigram F1 scores for NMT systems using full words and byte-pair encoded tokens. Scores are reported separately for the following classes: words in the vocabulary of both the full-word and BPE models (Full), words in the vocabulary of the full-word model that are split in the BPE model (Split), words outside the vocabulary of the full-word model but covered by its dictionary (Dict), words outside the vocabulary of the full-word model and its dictionary that should be translated (OOV-T), and words outside the vocabulary of the full-word model and its dictionary that should be passed through (OOV-P). All reported scores are averaged over 3 independent optimizer runs.

| | WMT | | | IWSLT | |
|---|---|---|---|---|---|
| | DE-EN | EN-FI | RO-EN | EN-FR | CS-EN |
| Vanilla | 30.2 | 11.8 | 26.4 | 33.2 | 20.2 |
| Recommended | 33.5 | 14.7 | 27.8 | 34.5 | 22.6 |
| +Ensemble | **35.8** | **17.3** | **30.3** | **37.3** | **25.5** |

Table 3: Test set BLEU scores for "vanilla" NMT (full words and standard Adam), and our recommended systems (byte pair encoding and annealing Adam, with and without ensembling). Scores for single models are averaged over 3 independent optimizer runs while scores for ensembles are the result of combining 3 runs.

| EN-FR | Adam | | +Annealing | | +Ensemble |
|---|---|---|---|---|---|
| | Word | BPE | Word | BPE | BPE |
| Baseline | 33.2 | 33.7 | 33.6 | 34.8 | 37.3 |
| Dropout | **33.9** | **33.9** | **34.5** | *34.7* | *37.2* |
| Lexicon Bias | **33.8** | **34.0** | **33.9** | *34.8* | *37.1* |
| Pre-Translation | – | **34.0** | – | **34.9** | *36.6* |
| Bootstrapping | **33.7** | **34.1** | **34.4** | **35.2** | **37.4** |

| CS-EN | Adam | | +Annealing | | +Ensemble |
|---|---|---|---|---|---|
| | Word | BPE | Word | BPE | BPE |
| Baseline | 20.2 | 22.1 | 21.0 | 23.0 | 25.5 |
| Dropout | **20.7** | **22.7** | **21.4** | **23.6** | **26.1** |
| Lexicon Bias | **20.7** | **22.5** | *20.6* | *22.7* | *25.2* |
| Pre-Translation | – | **23.1** | – | **23.8** | **25.8** |
| Bootstrapping | **20.7** | **23.2** | **21.6** | **23.6** | **26.2** |

Table 4: Test set BLEU scores for several published NMT extensions. Entries are evaluated with and without Adam annealing, byte pair encoding, and model ensembling. A bold score indicates improvement over the baseline while an italic score indicates no change or degradation. Scores for non-ensembles are averaged over 3 independent optimizer runs and ensembles are the result of combining 3 runs.

duce training time, some work ensembles different training checkpoints of the same model rather than using fully independent models (Jean et al., 2015; Sennrich et al., 2016a). While checkpoint ensembling is shown to be effective for improving BLEU scores under resource constraints, it does so with less diverse models. As discussed in recent work and demonstrated in our experiments in §6, model diversity is a key component in building strong NMT ensembles (Jean et al., 2015; Sennrich et al., 2016a; Farajian et al., 2016). For these reasons, we recommend evaluating new techniques on systems that ensemble multiple independently trained models for the most reliable results. Results showing both the effectiveness of ensembles and the importance of model diversity are included in the larger experiments conducted in the next section.

## 6 On Trustable Evaluation

### 6.1 Experimental Setup

In this section, we evaluate and discuss the effects that choice of baseline can have on experimental conclusions regarding neural MT systems. First, we build systems that include Adam with rate annealing, byte pair encoding, and independent model ensembling and compare them to the vanilla baselines described in §2.1. As shown in Table 3, combining these techniques leads to a consistent improvement of 4-5 BLEU points across all scenarios. These improvements are the result of addressing several underlying weaknesses of basic NMT models as described in previous sections, leading to systems that behave much closer to those deployed for real-world tasks.

Next, to empirically demonstrate the importance of evaluating new methods in the context of these stronger systems, we select several tech-

niques shown to improve NMT performance and compare their effects as baseline systems are iteratively strengthened. Focusing on English-French and Czech-English, we evaluate the following techniques with and without the proposed improvements, reporting results in Table 4:

**Dropout:** Apply the improved dropout technique for sequence models described by Gal and Ghahramani (2016) to LSTM layers with a rate of 0.2. We find this version to significantly outperform standard dropout.

**Lexicon bias:** Incorporate scores from a pretrained lexicon (`fast_align` model learned on the same data) directly as additional weights when selecting output words (Arthur et al., 2016). Target word lexicon scores are computed as weighted sums over source words based on attention scores.

**Pre-translation:** Translate source sentences with a traditional phrase-based system trained on the same data. Input for the neural system is the original source sentence concatenated with the PBMT output (Niehues et al., 2016). Input words are prefixed with either `s_` or `t_` to denote source or target language. We improve performance with a novel extension where word alignments are used to weave together source and PBMT output so that each original word is immediately followed by its suggested translation from the phrase-based system. As pre-translation doubles source vocabulary size and input length, we only apply it to sub-word systems to keep complexity reasonable.

**Data bootstrapping:** Expand training data by extracting phrase pairs (sub-sentence translation examples) and including them as additional training instances (Chen et al., 2016). We apply a novel extension where we train a phrase-based system and use it to re-translate the training data, providing a near-optimal phrase segmentation as a byproduct. We use these phrases in place of the heuristically chosen phrases in the original work, improving coverage and leading to more fine-grained translation examples.

### 6.2 Experimental Results

The immediately noticeable trend from Table 4 is that while all techniques improve basic systems, only a single technique, data bootstrapping, improves the fully strengthened system for both data sets (and barely so). This can be attributed to a mix of redundancy and incompatibility between the improvements we've discussed in previous sections and the techniques evaluated here.

Lexicon bias and pre-translation both incorporate scores from pre-trained models that are shown to improve handling of rare words. When NMT models are sub-optimally trained, they can benefit from the suggestions of a better-trained model. When full-word NMT models struggle to learn translations for infrequent words, they can learn to simply trust the lexical or phrase-based model. However, when annealing Adam and BPE alleviate these underlying problems, the neural model's accuracy can match or exceed that of the pre-trained model, making external scores either completely redundant or (in the worst case) harmful bias that must be overcome to produce correct translations. While pre-translation fares better than lexicon bias, it suffers a reversal in one scenario and a significant degradation in the other when moving from a single model to an ensemble. Even when bias from an external model improves translation, it does so at the cost of diversity by pushing the neural model's preferences toward those of the pre-trained model. These results further validate claims of the importance of diversity in model ensembles.

Applying dropout significantly improves all configurations of the Czech-English system and some configurations of the English-French system, leveling off with the strongest. This trend follows previous work showing that dropout combats overfitting of small data, though the point of inflection is worth noting (Sennrich et al., 2016a; Wu et al., 2016). Even though the English-French data is still relatively small (220K sentences), BPE leads to a smaller vocabulary of more general translation units, effectively reducing sparsity, while annealing Adam can avoid getting stuck in poor local optima. These techniques already lead to better generalization without the need for dropout. Finally, we can observe a few key properties of data bootstrapping, the best performing technique on fully strengthened systems. Unlike lexicon bias and pre-translation, it modifies only the training data, allowing "purely neural" models to be learned from random initialization points. This preserves model diversity, allowing ensembles to benefit as well as single models. Further, data bootstrapping is complementary to annealing Adam and BPE; better optimization and a more general vocabulary can make better use of the new training instances.

While evaluation on simple vanilla NMT systems would indicate that all of the techniques in this section lead to significant improvement for both data sets, only evaluation on systems using annealing Adam, byte pair encoding, and independent model ensembling reveals both the reversals of results on state-of-the-art systems and nuanced interactions between techniques that we have reported. Based on these results, we highly recommend evaluating new techniques on systems that are at least this strong and representative of those deployed for real-world use.

### 7 Conclusion

In this work, we have empirically demonstrated the effectiveness of Adam training with multiple restarts and step size annealing, byte pair encoding, and independent model ensembling both for improving BLEU scores and increasing the reliability of experimental results. Out of four previously published techniques for improving vanilla NMT, only one, data bootstrapping via phrase extraction, also improves a fully strengthened model across all scenarios. For these reasons, we recommend evaluating new model extensions and algorithms on NMT systems at least as strong as those we have described for maximally trustable results.

## References

Philip Arthur, Graham Neubig, and Satoshi Nakamura. 2016. Incorporating discrete translation lexicons into neural machine translation. In *Proceedings of the 2016 Conference on Empirical Methods in Natural Language Processing*. Association for Computational Linguistics, Austin, Texas, pages 1557–1567.

Dzmitry Bahdanau, Kyunghyun Cho, and Yoshua Bengio. 2015. Neural machine translation by jointly learning to align and translate. In *International Conference on Learning Representations*.

Ondřej Bojar, Rajen Chatterjee, Christian Federmann, Yvette Graham, Barry Haddow, Matthias Huck, Antonio Jimeno Yepes, Philipp Koehn, Varvara Logacheva, Christof Monz, Matteo Negri, Aurelie Neveol, Mariana Neves, Martin Popel, Matt Post, Raphael Rubino, Carolina Scarton, Lucia Specia, Marco Turchi, Karin Verspoor, and Marcos Zampieri. 2016. Findings of the 2016 conference on machine translation. In *Proceedings of the First Conference on Machine Translation*. Association for Computational Linguistics, Berlin, Germany, pages 131–198.

Denny Britz, Anna Goldie, Thang Luong, and Quoc Le. 2017. Massive exploration of neural machine translation architectures. *arXiv preprint arXiv:1703.03906* .

M Cettolo, J Niehues, S Stüker, L Bentivogli, R Cattoni, and M Federico. 2016. The iwslt 2016 evaluation campaign .

Mauro Cettolo, Christian Girardi, and Marcello Federico. 2012. Wit$^3$: Web inventory of transcribed and translated talks. In *Proceedings of the 16$^{th}$ Conference of the European Association for Machine Translation (EAMT)*. Trento, Italy, pages 261–268.

Wenhu Chen, Evgeny Matusov, Shahram Khadivi, and Jan-Thorsten Peter. 2016. Guided alignment training for topic-aware neural machine translation. *AMTA 2016, Vol.* page 121.

Jonathan H. Clark, Chris Dyer, Alon Lavie, and Noah A. Smith. 2011. Better hypothesis testing for statistical machine translation: Controlling for optimizer instability. In *Proceedings of the 49th Annual Meeting of the Association for Computational Linguistics: Human Language Technologies*. pages 176–181.

Josep Crego, Jungi Kim, Guillaume Klein, Anabel Rebollo, Kathy Yang, Jean Senellart, Egor Akhanov, Patrice Brunelle, Aurelien Coquard, Yongchao Deng, Satoshi Enoue, Chiyo Geiss, Joshua Johanson, Ardas Khalsa, Raoum Khiari, Byeongil Ko, Catherine Kobus, Jean Lorieux, Leidiana Martins, Dang-Chuan Nguyen, Alexandra Priori, Thomas Riccardi, Natalia Segal, Christophe Servan, Cyril Tiquet, Bo Wang, Jin Yang, Dakun Zhang, Jing Zhou, and Peter Zoldan. 2016. SYSTRAN's pure neural machine translation systems. *CoRR* abs/1610.05540.

Chris Dyer, Victor Chahuneau, and Noah A. Smith. 2013. A simple, fast, and effective reparameterization of ibm model 2. In *Proceedings of the 2013 Conference of the North American Chapter of the Association for Computational Linguistics: Human Language Technologies*. pages 644–648.

M Amin Farajian, Rajen Chatterjee, Costanza Conforti, Shahab Jalalvand, Vevake Balaraman, Mattia A Di Gangi, Duygu Ataman, Marco Turchi, Matteo Negri, and Marcello Federico. 2016. Fbks neural machine translation systems for iwslt 2016. In *Proceedings of the ninth International Workshop on Spoken Language Translation (IWSLT), Seattle, WA*.

Yarin Gal and Zoubin Ghahramani. 2016. A theoretically grounded application of dropout in recurrent neural networks. In D. D. Lee, M. Sugiyama, U. V. Luxburg, I. Guyon, and R. Garnett, editors, *Advances in Neural Information Processing Systems 29*, Curran Associates, Inc., pages 1019–1027.

Geoffrey Hinton, Oriol Vinyals, and Jeff Dean. 2015. Distilling the knowledge in a neural network. *arXiv preprint arXiv:1503.02531* .

Sébastien Jean, Kyunghyun Cho, Roland Memisevic, and Yoshua Bengio. 2015. On using very large target vocabulary for neural machine translation. In *Proceedings of the 53rd Annual Meeting of the Association for Computational Linguistics and the 7th International Joint Conference on Natural Language Processing (Volume 1: Long Papers)*. Association for Computational Linguistics, Beijing, China, pages 1–10.

Yoon Kim and Alexander M. Rush. 2016. Sequence-level knowledge distillation. In *Proceedings of the 2016 Conference on Empirical Methods in Natural Language Processing*. Association for Computational Linguistics, Austin, Texas, pages 1317–1327.

Diederik P. Kingma and Jimmy Ba. 2015. Adam: A method for stochastic optimization. In *Proceedings of the 3rd International Conference on Learning Representations (ICLR)*.

Adhiguna Kuncoro, Miguel Ballesteros, Lingpeng Kong, Chris Dyer, and Noah A. Smith. 2016. Distilling an ensemble of greedy dependency parsers into one mst parser. In *Proceedings of the 2016 Conference on Empirical Methods in Natural Language Processing*. Association for Computational Linguistics, Austin, Texas, pages 1744–1753.

Jason Lee, Kyunghyun Cho, and Thomas Hofmann. 2016. Fully character-level neural machine translation without explicit segmentation. *CoRR* abs/1610.03017.

Thang Luong, Ilya Sutskever, Quoc Le, Oriol Vinyals, and Wojciech Zaremba. 2015. Addressing the rare word problem in neural machine translation. In *Proceedings of the 53rd Annual Meeting of the Association for Computational Linguistics and the 7th International Joint Conference on Natural Language Processing (Volume 1: Long Papers)*. pages 11–19.

Graham Neubig. 2015. lamtram: A toolkit for language and translation modeling using neural networks. http://www.github.com/neubig/lamtram.

Graham Neubig, Chris Dyer, Yoav Goldberg, Austin Matthews, Waleed Ammar, Antonios Anastasopoulos, Miguel Ballesteros, David Chiang, Daniel Clothiaux, Trevor Cohn, Kevin Duh, Manaal Faruqui, Cynthia Gan, Dan Garrette, Yangfeng Ji, Lingpeng Kong, Adhiguna Kuncoro, Gaurav Kumar, Chaitanya Malaviya, Paul Michel, Yusuke Oda, Matthew Richardson, Naomi Saphra, Swabha Swayamdipta, and Pengcheng Yin. 2017. Dynet: The dynamic neural network toolkit. *arXiv preprint arXiv:1701.03980* .

Jan Niehues, Eunah Cho, Thanh-Le Ha, and Alex Waibel. 2016. Pre-translation for neural machine translation. *CoRR* abs/1610.05243.

Kishore Papineni, Salim Roukos, Todd Ward, and Wei-Jing Zhu. 2002. Bleu: a method for automatic evaluation of machine translation. In *Proceedings of 40th Annual Meeting of the Association for Computational Linguistics*. Association for Computational Linguistics, Philadelphia, Pennsylvania, USA, pages 311–318.

Rico Sennrich, Orhan Firat, Kyunghyun Cho, Alexandra Birch, Barry Haddow, Julian Hitschler, Marcin Junczys-Dowmunt, Samuel Läubli, Antonio Valerio Miceli Barone, Jozef Mokry, and Maria Nadejde. 2017. Nematus: a Toolkit for Neural Machine Translation. In *Proceedings of the Demonstrations at the 15th Conference of the European Chapter of the Association for Computational Linguistics*. Valencia, Spain.

Rico Sennrich, Barry Haddow, and Alexandra Birch. 2016a. Edinburgh neural machine translation systems for wmt 16. In *Proceedings of the First Conference on Machine Translation*. Association for Computational Linguistics, Berlin, Germany, pages 371–376.

Rico Sennrich, Barry Haddow, and Alexandra Birch. 2016b. Neural machine translation of rare words with subword units. In *Proceedings of the 54th Annual Meeting of the Association for Computational Linguistics (Volume 1: Long Papers)*. Association for Computational Linguistics, Berlin, Germany, pages 1715–1725.

Ilya Sutskever, Oriol Vinyals, and Quoc V Le. 2014. Sequence to sequence learning with neural networks. In *Advances in neural information processing systems*. pages 3104–3112.

Yonghui Wu, Mike Schuster, Zhifeng Chen, Quoc V. Le, Mohammad Norouzi, Wolfgang Macherey, Maxim Krikun, Yuan Cao, Qin Gao, Klaus Macherey, Jeff Klingner, Apurva Shah, Melvin Johnson, Xiaobing Liu, Lukasz Kaiser, Stephan Gouws, Yoshikiyo Kato, Taku Kudo, Hideto Kazawa, Keith Stevens, George Kurian, Nishant Patil, Wei Wang, Cliff Young, Jason Smith, Jason Riesa, Alex Rudnick, Oriol Vinyals, Greg Corrado, Macduff Hughes, and Jeffrey Dean. 2016. Google's neural machine translation system: Bridging the gap between human and machine translation. *CoRR* abs/1609.08144.

Matthew D. Zeiler. 2012. ADADELTA: an adaptive learning rate method. *CoRR* abs/1212.5701.

# Six Challenges for Neural Machine Translation

**Philipp Koehn**
Computer Science Department
Johns Hopkins University
`phi@jhu.edu`

**Rebecca Knowles**
Computer Science Department
Johns Hopkins University
`rknowles@jhu.edu`

## Abstract

We explore six challenges for neural machine translation: domain mismatch, amount of training data, rare words, long sentences, word alignment, and beam search. We show both deficiencies and improvements over the quality of phrase-based statistical machine translation.

## 1 Introduction

Neural machine translation has emerged as the most promising machine translation approach in recent years, showing superior performance on public benchmarks (Bojar et al., 2016) and rapid adoption in deployments by, e.g., Google (Wu et al., 2016), Systran (Crego et al., 2016), and WIPO (Junczys-Dowmunt et al., 2016). But there have also been reports of poor performance, such as the systems built under low-resource conditions in the DARPA LORELEI program.[1]

In this paper, we examine a number of challenges to neural machine translation (NMT) and give empirical results on how well the technology currently holds up, compared to traditional statistical machine translation (SMT).

We find that:

1. NMT systems have lower quality **out of domain**, to the point that they completely sacrifice adequacy for the sake of fluency.

2. NMT systems have a steeper learning curve with respect to the **amount of training data**, resulting in worse quality in low-resource settings, but better performance in high-resource settings.

3. NMT systems that operate at the sub-word level (e.g. with byte-pair encoding) perform better than SMT systems on extremely **low-frequency words**, but still show weakness in translating low-frequency words belonging to highly-inflected categories (e.g. verbs).

4. NMT systems have lower translation quality on very **long sentences**, but do comparably better up to a sentence length of about 60 words.

5. The attention model for NMT does not always fulfill the role of a **word alignment model**, but may in fact dramatically diverge.

6. **Beam search decoding** only improves translation quality for narrow beams and deteriorates when exposed to a larger search space.

We note a 7th challenge that we do not examine empirically: NMT systems are much less interpretable. The answer to the question of why the training data leads these systems to decide on specific word choices during decoding is buried in large matrices of real-numbered values. There is a clear need to develop better analytics for NMT.

Other studies have looked at the comparable performance of NMT and SMT systems. Bentivogli et al. (2016) considered different linguistic categories for English–German and Toral and Sánchez-Cartagena (2017) compared different broad aspects such as fluency and reordering for nine language directions.

## 2 Experimental Setup

We use common toolkits for neural machine translation (Nematus) and traditional phrase-based statistical machine translation (Moses) with common data sets, drawn from WMT and OPUS.

---

[1] `https://www.nist.gov/itl/iad/mig/lorehlt16-evaluations`



*Proceedings of the First Workshop on Neural Machine Translation*, pages 28–39,
Vancouver, Canada, August 4, 2017. ©2017 Association for Computational Linguistics

## 2.1 Neural Machine Translation

While a variety of neural machine translation approaches were initially proposed — such as the use of convolutional neural networks (Kalchbrenner and Blunsom, 2013) — practically all recent work has been focused on the attention-based encoder-decoder model (Bahdanau et al., 2015).

We use the toolkit Nematus[2] (Sennrich et al., 2017) which has been shown to give state-of-the-art results (Sennrich et al., 2016a) at the WMT 2016 evaluation campaign (Bojar et al., 2016).

Unless noted otherwise, we use default settings, such as beam search and single model decoding. The training data is processed with byte-pair encoding (Sennrich et al., 2016b) into subwords to fit a 50,000 word vocabulary limit.

## 2.2 Statistical Machine Translation

Our machine translation systems are trained using Moses[3] (Koehn et al., 2007). We build phrase-based systems using standard features that are commonly used in recent system submissions to WMT (Williams et al., 2016; Ding et al., 2016a).

While we use the shorthand SMT for these phrase-based systems, we note that there are other statistical machine translation approaches such as hierarchical phrase-based models (Chiang, 2007) and syntax-based models (Galley et al., 2004, 2006) that have been shown to give superior performance for language pairs such as Chinese–English and German–English.

## 2.3 Data Conditions

We carry out our experiments on English–Spanish and German–English. For these language pairs, large training data sets are available. We use datasets from the shared translation task organized alongside the Conference on Machine Translation (WMT)[4]. For the domain experiments, we use the OPUS corpus[5] (Tiedemann, 2012).

Except for the domain experiments, we use the WMT test sets composed of news stories, which are characterized by a broad range of topic, formal language, relatively long sentences (about 30 words on average), and high standards for grammar, orthography, and style.

| Corpus | Words | Sentences | W/S |
|---|---|---|---|
| Law (Acquis) | 18,128,173 | 715,372 | 25.3 |
| Medical (EMEA) | 14,301,472 | 1,104,752 | 12.9 |
| IT | 3,041,677 | 337,817 | 9.0 |
| Koran (Tanzil) | 9,848,539 | 480,421 | 20.5 |
| Subtitles | 114,371,754 | 13,873,398 | 8.2 |

Table 1: Corpora used to train domain-specific systems, taken from the OPUS repository. IT corpora are GNOME, KDE, PHP, Ubuntu, and OpenOffice.

## 3 Challenges

### 3.1 Domain Mismatch

A known challenge in translation is that in different domains,[6] words have different translations and meaning is expressed in different styles. Hence, a crucial step in developing machine translation systems targeted at a specific use case is domain adaptation. We expect that methods for domain adaptation will be developed for NMT. A currently popular approach is to train a general domain system, followed by training on in-domain data for a few epochs (Luong and Manning, 2015; Freitag and Al-Onaizan, 2016).

Often, large amounts of training data are only available out of domain, but we still seek to have robust performance. To test how well NMT and SMT hold up, we trained five different systems using different corpora obtained from OPUS (Tiedemann, 2012). An additional system was trained on all the training data. Statistics about corpus sizes are shown in Table 1. Note that these domains are quite distant from each other, much more so than, say, Europarl, TED Talks, News Commentary, and Global Voices.

We trained both SMT and NMT systems for all domains. All systems were trained for German-English, with tuning and test sets sub-sampled from the data (these were not used in training). A common byte-pair encoding is used for all training runs.

See Figure 1 for results. While the in-domain NMT and SMT systems are similar (NMT is better for IT and Subtitles, SMT is better for Law, Medical, and Koran), the out-of-domain performance for the NMT systems is worse in almost all cases, sometimes dramatically so. For instance the Med-

---

[2]https://github.com/rsennrich/nematus/
[3]http://www.stat.org/moses/
[4]http://www.statmt.org/wmt17/
[5]http://opus.lingfil.uu.se/

[6]We use the customary definition of domain in machine translation: a *domain* is defined by a corpus from a specific source, and may differ from other *domains* in topic, genre, style, level of formality, etc.

| System ↓ | Law | | Medical | | IT | | Koran | | Subtitles | |
|---|---|---|---|---|---|---|---|---|---|---|
| All Data | 30.5 | 32.8 | 45.1 | 42.2 | 35.3 | 44.7 | 17.9 | 17.9 | 26.4 | 20.8 |
| Law | 31.1 | 34.4 | 12.1 | 18.2 | 3.5 | 6.9 | 1.3 | 2.2 | 2.8 | 6.0 |
| Medical | 3.9 | 10.2 | 39.4 | 43.5 | 2.0 | 8.5 | 0.6 | 2.0 | 1.4 | 5.8 |
| IT | 1.9 | 3.7 | 6.5 | 5.3 | 42.1 | 39.8 | 1.8 | 1.6 | 3.9 | 4.7 |
| Koran | 0.4 | 1.8 | 0.0 | 2.1 | 0.0 | 2.3 | 15.9 | 18.8 | 1.0 | 5.5 |
| Subtitles | 7.0 | 9.9 | 9.3 | 17.8 | 9.2 | 13.6 | 9.0 | 8.4 | 25.9 | 22.1 |

Figure 1: Quality of systems (BLEU), when trained on one domain (rows) and tested on another domain (columns). Comparably, NMT systems (left bars) show more degraded performance out of domain.

ical system leads to a BLEU score of 3.9 (NMT) vs. 10.2 (SMT) on the Law test set.

Figure 2 displays an example. When translating the sentence *Schaue um dich herum.* (reference: *Look around you.*) from the Subtitles corpus, we see mostly non-sensical and completely unrelated output from the NMT system. For instance, the translation from the IT system is *Switches to paused.*

Note that the output of the NMT system is often quite fluent (e.g., *Take heed of your own souls.*) but completely unrelated to the input, while the SMT output betrays its difficulties with coping with the out-of-domain input by leaving some words untranslated (e.g., *Schaue by dich around.*). This is of particular concern when MT is used for information gisting — the user will be mislead by hallucinated content in the NMT output.

## 3.2 Amount of Training Data

A well-known property of statistical systems is that increasing amounts of training data lead to better results. In SMT systems, we have previously observed that doubling the amount of training data gives a fixed increase in BLEU scores. This holds true for both parallel and monolingual data (Turchi et al., 2008; Irvine and Callison-Burch, 2013).

| Source | Schaue um dich herum. |
|---|---|
| Ref. | Look around you. |
| All | NMT: Look around you.<br>SMT: Look around you. |
| Law | NMT: Sughum gravecorn.<br>SMT: In order to implement dich Schaue . |
| Medical | NMT: EMEA / MB / 049 / 01-EN-Final Work progamme for 2002<br>SMT: Schaue by dich around . |
| IT | NMT: Switches to paused.<br>SMT: To Schaue by itself . \t \t |
| Koran | NMT: Take heed of your own souls.<br>SMT: And you see. |
| Subtitles | NMT: Look around you.<br>SMT: Look around you . |

Figure 2: Examples for the translation of a sentence from the Subtitles corpus, when translated with systems trained on different corpora. Performance out-of-domain is dramatically worse for NMT.

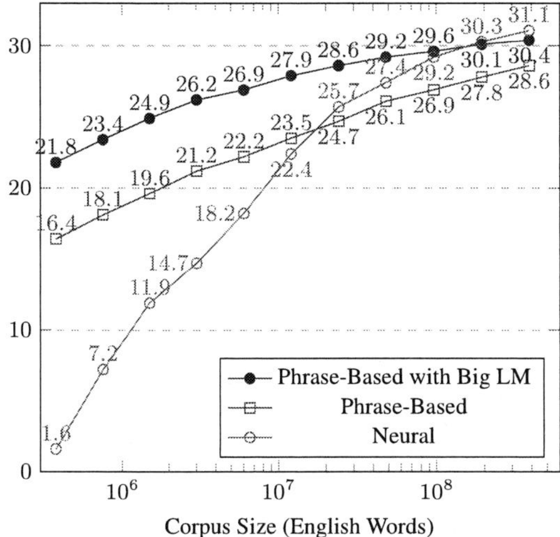


Figure 3: BLEU scores for English-Spanish systems trained on 0.4 million to 385.7 million words of parallel data. Quality for NMT starts much lower, outperforms SMT at about 15 million words, and even beats a SMT system with a big 2 billion word in-domain language model under high-resource conditions.

| Src: | A Republican strategy to counter the re-election of Obama |
| --- | --- |
| $\frac{1}{1024}$ | Un órgano de coordinación para el anuncio de libre determinación |
| $\frac{1}{512}$ | Lista de una estrategia para luchar contra la elección de hojas de Ohio |
| $\frac{1}{256}$ | Explosión realiza una estrategia divisiva de luchar contra las elecciones de autor |
| $\frac{1}{128}$ | Una estrategia republicana para la eliminación de la reelección de Obama |
| $\frac{1}{64}$ | Estrategia siria para contrarrestar la reelección del Obama . |
| $\frac{1}{32}+$ | Una estrategia republicana para contrarrestar la reelección de Obama |

Figure 4: Translations of the first sentence of the test set using NMT system trained on varying amounts of training data. Under low resource conditions, NMT produces fluent output unrelated to the input.

How do the data needs of SMT and NMT compare? NMT promises both to generalize better (exploiting word similary in embeddings) and condition on larger context (entire input and all prior output words).

We built English-Spanish systems on WMT data,[7] about 385.7 million English words paired with Spanish. To obtain a learning curve, we used $\frac{1}{1024}$, $\frac{1}{512}$, ..., $\frac{1}{2}$, and all of the data. For SMT, the language model was trained on the Spanish part of each subset, respectively. In addition to a NMT and SMT system trained on each subset, we also used all additionally provided monolingual data for a big language model in contrastive SMT systems.

Results are shown in Figure 3. NMT exhibits a much steeper learning curve, starting with abysmal results (BLEU score of 1.6 vs. 16.4 for $\frac{1}{1024}$ of the data), outperforming SMT 25.7 vs. 24.7 with $\frac{1}{16}$ of the data (24.1 million words), and even beating the SMT system with a big language model with the full data set (31.1 for NMT, 28.4 for SMT, 30.4 for SMT+BigLM).

The contrast between the NMT and SMT learning curves is quite striking. While NMT is able to exploit increasing amounts of training data more effectively, it is unable to get off the ground with training corpus sizes of a few million words or less.

To illustrate this, see Figure 4. With $\frac{1}{1024}$ of the training data, the output is completely unrelated to the input, some key words are properly translated with $\frac{1}{512}$ and $\frac{1}{256}$ of the data (*estrategia* for *strategy*, *elección* or *elecciones* for *election*), and starting with $\frac{1}{64}$ the translations become respectable.

### 3.3 Rare Words

Conventional wisdom states that neural machine translation models perform particularly poorly on rare words, (Luong et al., 2015; Sennrich et al., 2016b; Arthur et al., 2016) due in part to the smaller vocabularies used by NMT systems. We examine this claim by comparing performance on rare word translation between NMT and SMT systems of similar quality for German–English and find that NMT systems actually outperform SMT systems on translation of very infrequent words. However, both NMT and SMT systems do continue to have difficulty translating some infrequent words, particularly those belonging to highly-inflected categories.

For the neural machine translation model, we use a publicly available model[8] with the training settings of Edinburgh's WMT submission (Sennrich et al., 2016a). This was trained using Ne-

---

[7]Spanish was last represented in 2013, we used data from `http://statmt.org/wmt13/translation-task.html`

[8]`https://github.com/rsennrich/wmt16-scripts/`

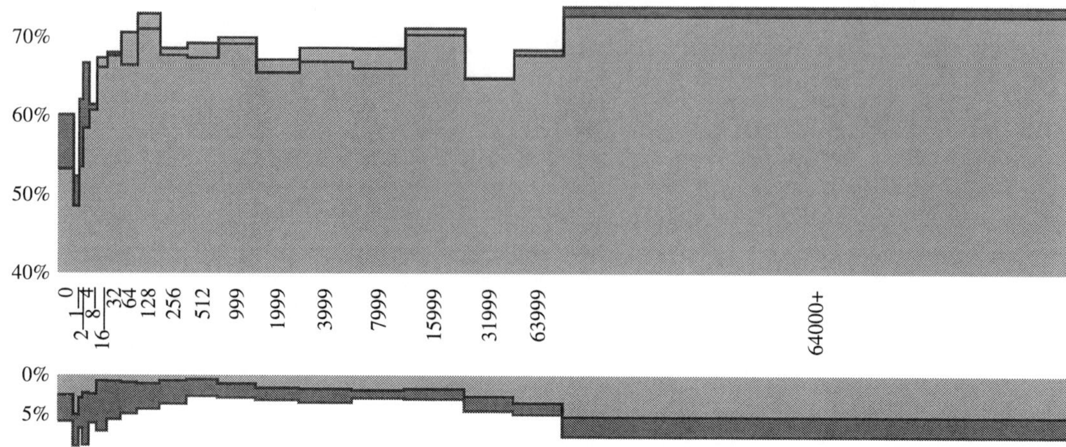


Figure 5: Precision of translation and deletion rates by source words type. SMT (light blue) and NMT (dark green). The horizontal axis represents the corpus frequency of the source types, with the axis labels showing the upper end of the bin. Bin width is proportional to the number of word types in that frequency range. The upper part of the graph shows the precision averaged across all word types in the bin. The lower part shows the proportion of source tokens in the bin that were deleted.

matus[9] (Sennrich et al., 2017), with byte-pair encodings (Sennrich et al., 2016b) to allow for open-vocabulary NMT.

The phrase-based model that we used was trained using Moses (Koehn et al., 2007), and the training data and parameters match those described in Johns Hopkins University's submission to the WMT shared task (Ding et al., 2016b).

Both models have case-sensitive BLEU scores of 34.5 on the WMT 2016 news test set (for the NMT model, this reflects the BLEU score resulting from translation with a beam size of 1). We use a single corpus for computing our lexical frequency counts (a concatenation of Common Crawl, Europarl, and News Commentary).

We follow the approach described by Koehn and Haddow (2012) for examining the effect of source word frequency on translation accuracy.[10]

The overall average precision is quite similar between the NMT and SMT systems, with the SMT system scoring 70.1% overall and the NMT system scoring 70.3%. This reflects the similar overall quality of the MT systems. Figure 5 gives a detailed breakdown. The values above the horizontal axis represent precisions, while the lower portion represents what proportion of the words were deleted. The first item of note is that the NMT system has an overall higher proportion of deleted words. Of the 64379 words examined, the NMT system is estimated to have deleted 3769 of them, while the SMT system deleted 2274. Both the NMT and SMT systems delete very frequent and very infrequent words at higher proportions than words that fall into the middle range. Across frequencies, the NMT systems delete a higher proportion of words than the SMT system does. (The related issue of translation length is discussed in more detail in Section 3.4.)

The next interesting observation is what happens with unknown words (words which were never observed in the training corpus). The SMT system translates these correctly 53.2% of the time, while the NMT system translates them correctly 60.1% of the time. This is reflected in Figure 5, where the SMT system shows a steep curve

---

[9]https://github.com/rsennrich/nematus/

[10]First, we automatically align the source sentence and the machine translation output. We use fast-align (Dyer et al., 2013) to align the full training corpus (source and reference) along with the test source and MT output. We use the suggested standard options for alignment and then symmetrize the alignment with grow-diag-final-and.

Each source word is either unaligned ("dropped") or aligned to one or more target language words. For each target word to which the source word is aligned, we check if that target word appears in the reference translation. If the target word appears the same number of times in the MT output as in the reference, we award that alignment a score of one. If the target word appears more times in the MT output than in the reference, we award fractional credit. If the target word does not appear in the reference, we award zero credit.

We then average these scores over the full set of target words aligned to the given source word to compute the precision for that source word. Source words can then be binned by frequency and average translation precisions can be computed.

| Label | Unobserved | Observed Once |
|---|---|---|
| Adjective | 4 | 10 |
| Named Entity | 40 | 42 |
| Noun | 35 | 35 |
| Number | 12 | 4 |
| Verb | 3 | 6 |
| Other | 6 | 3 |

Table 2: Breakdown of the first 100 tokens that were unobserved in training or observed once in training, by hand-annotated category.

| Src. | (1) ... **choreographiertes** Gesamtkunstwerk ...<br>(2) ... die Polizei ihn **einkesselte**. |
|---|---|
| BPE | (1) **chore@@ ograph@@ iertes**<br>(2) **ein@@ kes@@ sel@@ te** |
| NMT | (1) ... **choreographed** overall artwork ...<br>(2) ... police **stabbed** him. |
| SMT | (1) ... **choreographiertes** total work of art ...<br>(2) ... police **einkesselte** him. |
| Ref. | (1) ... **choreographed** complete work of art ...<br>(2) ... police **closed in on** him. |

Figure 6: Examples of words that were unobserved in the training corpus, their byte-pair encodings, and their translations.

up from the unobserved words, while the NMT system does not see a great jump.

Both SMT and NMT systems actually have their worst performance on words that were observed a single time in the training corpus, dropping to 48.6% and 52.2%, respectively; even worse than for unobserved words. Table 2 shows a breakdown of the categories of words that were unobserved in the training corpus or observed only once. The most common categories across both are named entity (including entity and location names) and nouns. The named entities can often be passed through unchanged (for example, the surname "Elabdellaoui" is broken into "E@@ lab@@ d@@ ell@@ a@@ oui" by the byte-pair encoding and is correctly passed through unchanged by both the NMT and SMT systems). Many of the nouns are compound nouns; when these are correctly translated, it may be attributed to compound-splitting (SMT) or byte-pair encoding (NMT). The factored SMT system also has access to the stemmed form of words, which can also play a similar role to byte-pair encoding in enabling translation of unobserved inflected forms (e.g. adjectives, verbs). Unsurprisingly, there are many numbers that were unobserved in the training data; these tend to be translated correctly (with occasional errors due to formatting of commas and periods, resolvable by post-processing).

The categories which involve more extensive inflection (adjectives and verbs) are arguably the most interesting. Adjectives and verbs have worse accuracy rates and higher deletion rates than nouns across most word frequencies. We show examples in Figure 6 of situations where the NMT system succeeds and fails, and contrast it with the failures of the SMT system. In Example 1, the NMT system successfully translates the unobserved adjective *choreographiertes* (choreographed), while the SMT system does not. In Example 2, the SMT system simply passes the German verb

*einkesselte* (closed in on) unchanged into the output, while the NMT system fails silently, selecting the fluent-sounding but semantically inappropriate "stabbed" instead.

While there remains room for improvement, NMT systems (at least those using byte-pair encoding) perform better on very low-frequency words then SMT systems do. Byte-pair encoding is sometimes sufficient (much like stemming or compound-splitting) to allow the successful translation of rare words even though it does not necessarily split words at morphological boundaries. As with the fluent-sounding but semantically inappropriate examples from domain-mismatch, NMT may sometimes fail similarly when it encounters unknown words even in-domain.

### 3.4 Long Sentences

A well-known flaw of early encoder-decoder NMT models was the inability to properly translate long sentences (Cho et al., 2014; Pouget-Abadie et al., 2014). The introduction of the attention model remedied this problem somewhat. But how well?

We used the large English-Spanish system from the learning curve experiments (Section 3.2), and used it to translate a collection of news test sets from the WMT shared tasks. We broke up these sets into buckets based on source sentence length (1-9 subword tokens, 10-19 subword tokens, etc.) and computed corpus-level BLEU scores for each.

Figure 7 shows the results. While overall NMT is better than SMT, the SMT system outperforms NMT on sentences of length 60 and higher. Quality for the two systems is relatively close, except for the very long sentences (80 and more tokens). The quality of the NMT system is dramatically lower for these since it produces too short translations (length ratio 0.859, opposed to 1.024).

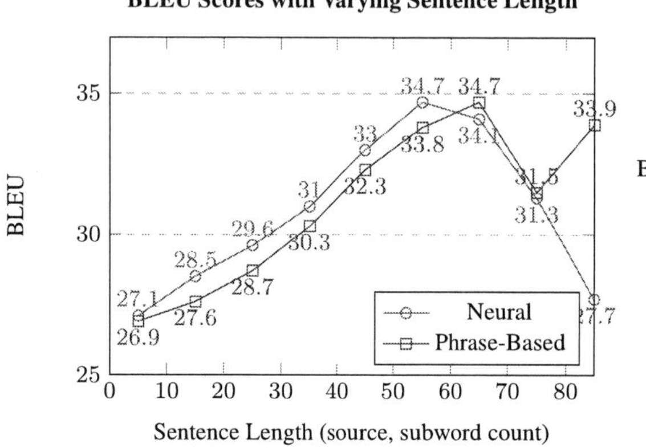


Figure 7: Quality of translations based on sentence length. SMT outperforms NMT for sentences longer than 60 subword tokens. For very long sentences (80+) quality is much worse due to too short output.

### 3.5 Word Alignment

The key contribution of the attention model in neural machine translation (Bahdanau et al., 2015) was the imposition of an alignment of the output words to the input words. This takes the shape of a probability distribution over the input words which is used to weigh them in a bag-of-words representation of the input sentence.

Arguably, this attention model does not functionally play the role of a word alignment between the source in the target, at least not in the same way as its analog in statistical machine translation. While in both cases, alignment is a latent variable that is used to obtain probability distributions over words or phrases, arguably the attention model has a broader role. For instance, when translating a verb, attention may also be paid to its subject and object since these may disambiguate it. To further complicate matters, the word representations are products of bidirectional gated recurrent neural networks that have the effect that each word representation is informed by the entire sentence context.

But there is a clear need for an alignment mechanism between source and target words. For instance, prior work used the alignments provided by the attention model to interpolate word translation decisions with traditional probabilistic dictionaries (Arthur et al., 2016), for the introduction of coverage and fertility models (Tu et al., 2016), etc.

But is the attention model in fact the proper

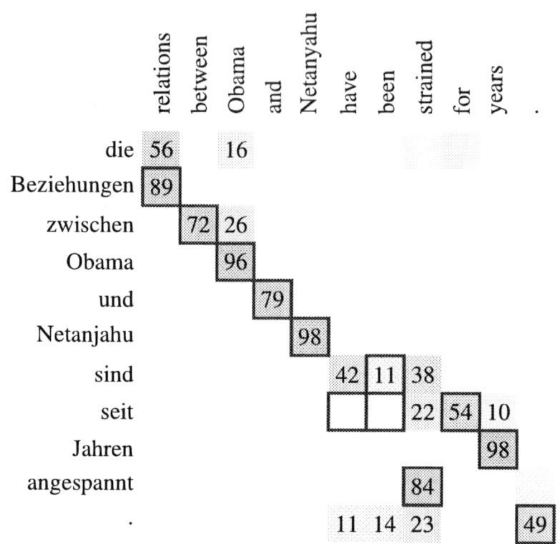

Figure 8: Word alignment for English–German: comparing the attention model states (green boxes with probability in percent if over 10) with alignments obtained from fast-align (blue outlines).

means? To examine this, we compare the soft alignment matrix (the sequence of attention vectors) with word alignments obtained by traditional word alignment methods. We use incremental fast-align (Dyer et al., 2013) to align the input and output of the neural machine system.

See Figure 8 for an illustration. We compare the word attention states (green boxes) with the word alignments obtained with fast align (blue outlines). For most words, these match up pretty well. Both attention states and fast-align alignment points are a bit fuzzy around the function words *have-been/sind*.

However, the attention model may settle on alignments that do not correspond with our intuition or alignment points obtained with fast-align. See Figure 9 for the reverse language direction, German–English. All the alignment points appear to be off by one position. We are not aware of any intuitive explanation for this divergent behavior — the translation quality is high for both systems.

We measure how well the soft alignment (attention model) of the NMT system match the alignments of fast-align with two metrics:

- a **match score** that checks for each output if the aligned input word according to fast-align is indeed the input word that received the highest attention probability, and

- a **probability mass score** that sums up the

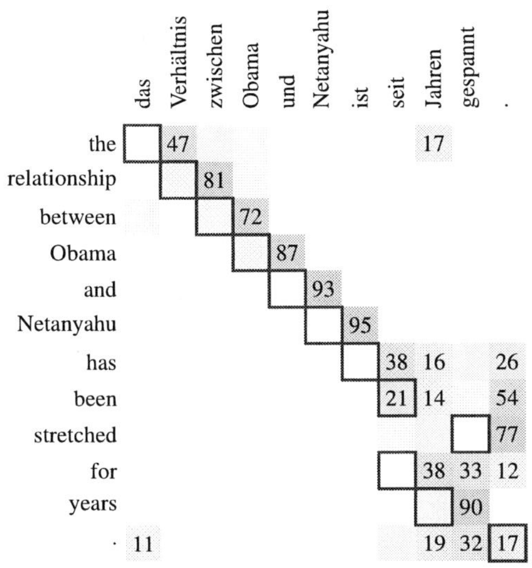



Figure 9: Mismatch between attention states and desired word alignments (German–English).

probability mass given to each alignment point obtained from fast-align.

In these scores, we have to handle byte pair encoding and many-to-many alignments[11]

In out experiment, we use the neural machine translation models provided by Edinburgh[12] (Sennrich et al., 2016a). We run fast-align on the same parallel data sets to obtain alignment models and used them to align the input and output of the NMT system. Table 3 shows alignment scores for the systems. The results suggest that, while drastic, the divergence for German–English is an outlier. We note, however, that we have seen such large a divergence also under different data conditions.

Note that the attention model may produce better word alignments by guided alignment training (Chen et al., 2016; Liu et al., 2016) where supervised word alignments (such as the ones produced by fast-align) are provided to model training.

---

[11](1) NMT operates on subwords, but fast-align is run on full words. (2) If an input word is split into subwords by byte pair encoding, then we add their attention scores. (3) If an output word is split into subwords, then we take the average of their attention vectors. (4) The match scores and probability mass scores are computed as average over output word-level scores. (5) If an output word has no fast-align alignment point, it is ignored in this computation. (6) If an output word is fast-aligned to multiple input words, then (6a) for the match score: count it as correct if the $n$ aligned words among the top $n$ highest scoring words according to attention and (6b) for the probability mass score: add up their attention scores.

[12]https://github.com/rsennrich/wmt16-scripts

| Language Pair | Match | Prob. |
|---|---|---|
| German–English | 14.9% | 16.0% |
| English–German | 77.2% | 63.2% |
| Czech–English | 78.0% | 63.3% |
| English–Czech | 76.1% | 59.7% |
| Russian–English | 72.5% | 65.0% |
| English–Russian | 73.4% | 64.1% |

Table 3: Scores indicating overlap between attention probabilities and alignments obtained with fast-align.

### 3.6 Beam Search

The task of decoding is to find the full sentence translation with the highest probability. In statistical machine translation, this problem has been addressed with heuristic search techniques that explore a subset of the space of possible translation. A common feature of these search techniques is a beam size parameter that limits the number of partial translations maintained per input word.

There is typically a straightforward relationship between this beam size parameter and the model score of resulting translations and also their quality score (e.g., BLEU). While there are diminishing returns for increasing the beam parameter, typically improvements in these scores can be expected with larger beams.

Decoding in neural translation models can be set up in similar fashion. When predicting the next output word, we may not only commit to the highest scoring word prediction but also maintain the next best scoring words in a list of partial translations. We record with each partial translation the word translation probabilities (obtained from the softmax), extend each partial translation with subsequent word predictions and accumulate these scores. Since the number of partial translation explodes exponentially with each new output word, we prune them down to a beam of highest scoring partial translations.

As in traditional statistical machine translation decoding, increasing the beam size allows us to explore a larger set of the space of possible translation and hence find translations with better model scores.

However, as Figure 10 illustrates, increasing the beam size does not consistently improve translation quality. In fact, in almost all cases, worse translations are found beyond an optimal beam size setting (we are using again Edinburgh's WMT

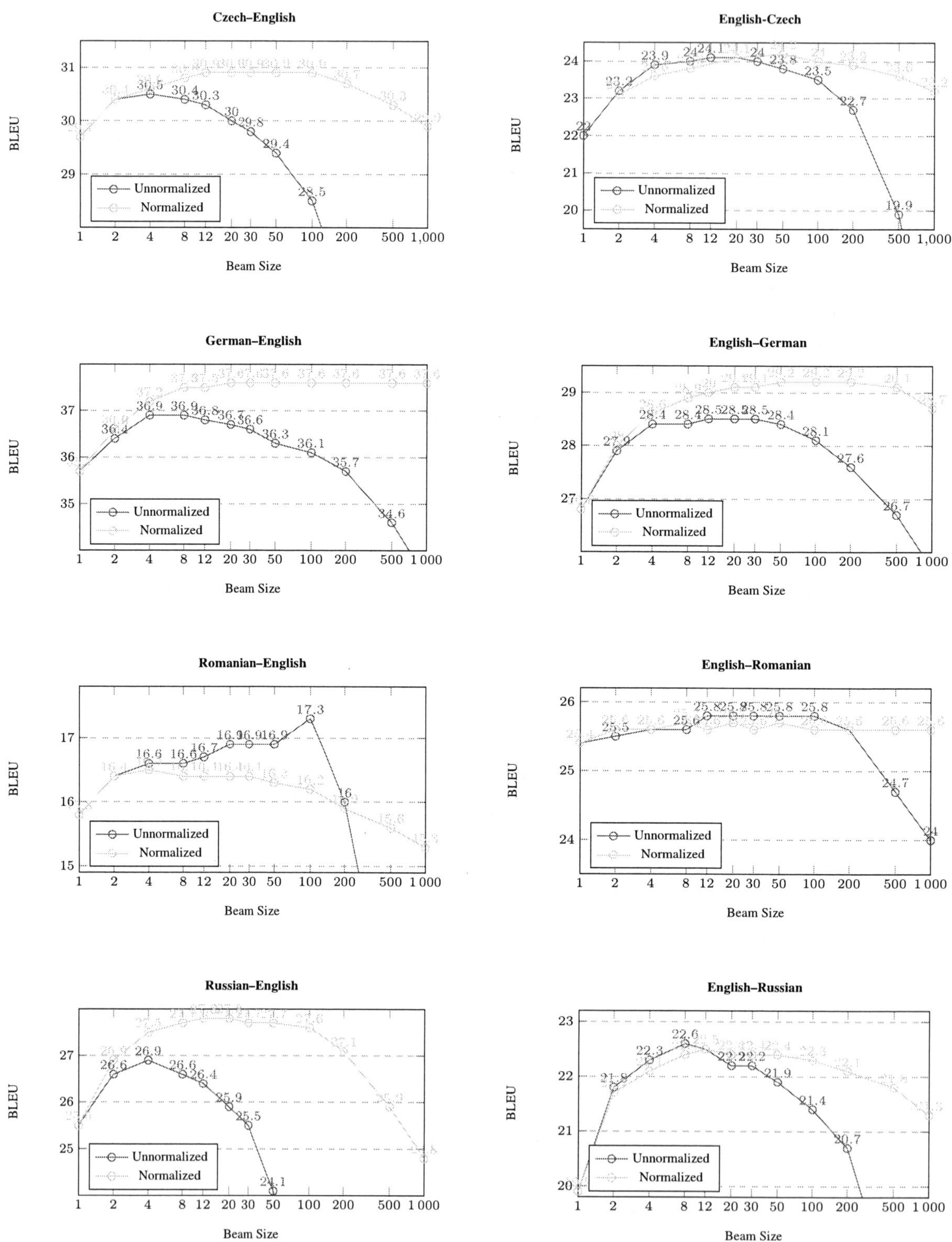

Figure 10: Translation quality with varying beam sizes. For large beams, quality decreases, especially when not normalizing scores by sentence length.

2016 systems). The optimal beam size varies from 4 (e.g., Czech–English) to around 30 (English–Romanian).

Normalizing sentence level model scores by length of the output alleviates the problem somewhat and also leads to better optimal quality in most cases (5 of the 8 language pairs investigated). Optimal beam sizes are in the range of 30–50 in almost all cases, but quality still drops with larger beams. The main cause of deteriorating quality are shorter translations under wider beams.

## 4 Conclusions

We showed that, despite its recent successes, neural machine translation still has to overcome various challenges, most notably performance out-of-domain and under low resource conditions. We hope that this paper motivates research to address these challenges.

What a lot of the problems have in common is that the neural translation models do not show robust behavior when confronted with conditions that differ significantly from training conditions — may it be due to limited exposure to training data, unusual input in case of out-of-domain test sentences, or unlikely initial word choices in beam search. The solution to these problems may hence lie in a more general approach of training that steps outside optimizing single word predictions given perfectly matching prior sequences.

## Acknowledgment

This work was partially supported by a Amazon Research Award (to the first author) and a National Science Foundation Graduate Research Fellowship under Grant No. DGE-1232825 (to the second author).

## References

Philip Arthur, Graham Neubig, and Satoshi Nakamura. 2016. Incorporating discrete translation lexicons into neural machine translation. In *Proceedings of the 2016 Conference on Empirical Methods in Natural Language Processing*. Association for Computational Linguistics, Austin, Texas, pages 1557–1567. https://aclweb.org/anthology/D16-1162.

Dzmitry Bahdanau, Kyunghyun Cho, and Yoshua Bengio. 2015. Neural machine translation by jointly learning to align and translate. In *ICLR*. http://arxiv.org/pdf/1409.0473v6.pdf.

Luisa Bentivogli, Arianna Bisazza, Mauro Cettolo, and Marcello Federico. 2016. Neural versus phrase-based machine translation quality: a case study. In *Proceedings of the 2016 Conference on Empirical Methods in Natural Language Processing*. Association for Computational Linguistics, Austin, Texas, pages 257–267. https://aclweb.org/anthology/D16-1025.

Ondřej Bojar, Rajen Chatterjee, Christian Federmann, Yvette Graham, Barry Haddow, Matthias Huck, Antonio Jimeno Yepes, Philipp Koehn, Varvara Logacheva, Christof Monz, Matteo Negri, Aurelie Neveol, Mariana Neves, Martin Popel, Matt Post, Raphael Rubino, Carolina Scarton, Lucia Specia, Marco Turchi, Karin Verspoor, and Marcos Zampieri. 2016. Findings of the 2016 conference on machine translation. In *Proceedings of the First Conference on Machine Translation*. Association for Computational Linguistics, Berlin, Germany, pages 131–198. http://www.aclweb.org/anthology/W/W16/W16-2301.

Wenhu Chen, Evgeny Matusov, Shahram Khadivi, and Jan-Thorsten Peter. 2016. Guided alignment training for topic-aware neural machine translation. *CoRR* abs/1607.01628. http://arxiv.org/abs/1607.01628.

David Chiang. 2007. Hierarchical phrase-based translation. *Computational Linguistics* 33(2). http://www.aclweb.org/anthology-new/J/J07/J07-2003.pdf.

Kyunghyun Cho, Bart van Merrienboer, Dzmitry Bahdanau, and Yoshua Bengio. 2014. On the properties of neural machine translation: Encoder–decoder approaches. In *Proceedings of SSST-8, Eighth Workshop on Syntax, Semantics and Structure in Statistical Translation*. Association for Computational Linguistics, Doha, Qatar, pages 103–111. http://www.aclweb.org/anthology/W14-4012.

Josep Maria Crego, Jungi Kim, Guillaume Klein, Anabel Rebollo, Kathy Yang, Jean Senellart, Egor Akhanov, Patrice Brunelle, Aurelien Coquard, Yongchao Deng, Satoshi Enoue, Chiyo Geiss, Joshua Johanson, Ardas Khalsa, Raoum Khiari, Byeongil Ko, Catherine Kobus, Jean Lorieux, Leidiana Martins, Dang-Chuan Nguyen, Alexandra Priori, Thomas Riccardi, Natalia Segal, Christophe Servan, Cyril Tiquet, Bo Wang, Jin Yang, Dakun Zhang, Jing Zhou, and Peter Zoldan. 2016. Systran's pure neural machine translation systems. *CoRR* abs/1610.05540. http://arxiv.org/abs/1610.05540.

Shuoyang Ding, Kevin Duh, Huda Khayrallah, Philipp Koehn, and Matt Post. 2016a. The jhu machine translation systems for wmt 2016. In *Proceedings of the First Conference on Machine Translation*. Association for Computational Linguistics, Berlin, Germany, pages 272–280. http://www.aclweb.org/anthology/W/W16/W16-2310.

Shuoyang Ding, Kevin Duh, Huda Khayrallah, Philipp Koehn, and Matt Post. 2016b. The JHU machine translation systems for WMT 2016. In *Proceedings of the First Conference on Machine Translation (WMT)*.

Chris Dyer, Victor Chahuneau, and Noah A. Smith. 2013. A simple, fast, and effective reparameterization of ibm model 2. In *Proceedings of the 2013 Conference of the North American Chapter of the Association for Computational Linguistics: Human Language Technologies*. Association for Computational Linguistics, Atlanta, Georgia, pages 644–648. http://www.aclweb.org/anthology/N13-1073.

Markus Freitag and Yaser Al-Onaizan. 2016. Fast domain adaptation for neural machine translation. *arXiv preprint arXiv:1612.06897* .

Michel Galley, Jonathan Graehl, Kevin Knight, Daniel Marcu, Steve DeNeefe, Wei Wang, and Ignacio Thayer. 2006. Scalable inference and training of context-rich syntactic translation models. In *Proceedings of the 21st International Conference on Computational Linguistics and 44th Annual Meeting of the Association for Computational Linguistics*. Association for Computational Linguistics, Sydney, Australia, pages 961–968. http://www.aclweb.org/anthology/P/P06/P06-1121.

Michel Galley, Mark Hopkins, Kevin Knight, and Daniel Marcu. 2004. What's in a translation rule? In *Proceedings of the Joint Conference on Human Language Technologies and the Annual Meeting of the North American Chapter of the Association of Computational Linguistics (HLT-NAACL)*. http://www.aclweb.org/anthology/N04-1035.pdf.

Ann Irvine and Chris Callison-Burch. 2013. Combining bilingual and comparable corpora for low resource machine translation. In *Proceedings of the Eighth Workshop on Statistical Machine Translation*. Association for Computational Linguistics, Sofia, Bulgaria, pages 262–270. http://www.aclweb.org/anthology/W13-2233.

Marcin Junczys-Dowmunt, Tomasz Dwojak, and Hieu Hoang. 2016. Is neural machine translation ready for deployment? a case study on 30 translation directions. In *Proceedings of the International Workshop on Spoken Language Translation (IWSLT)*. http://workshop2016.iwslt.org/downloads/IWSLT_2016_paper_4.pdf.

Nal Kalchbrenner and Phil Blunsom. 2013. Recurrent continuous translation models. In *Proceedings of the 2013 Conference on Empirical Methods in Natural Language Processing*. Association for Computational Linguistics, Seattle, Washington, USA, pages 1700–1709. http://www.aclweb.org/anthology/D13-1176.

Philipp Koehn and Barry Haddow. 2012. Interpolated backoff for factored translation models. In *Proceedings of the Tenth Conference of the Association for Machine Translation in the Americas (AMTA)*.

Philipp Koehn, Hieu Hoang, Alexandra Birch, Chris Callison-Burch, Marcello Federico, Nicola Bertoldi, Brooke Cowan, Wade Shen, Christine Moran, Richard Zens, Christopher J. Dyer, Ondřej Bojar, Alexandra Constantin, and Evan Herbst. 2007. Moses: Open source toolkit for statistical machine translation. In *Proceedings of the 45th Annual Meeting of the Association for Computational Linguistics Companion Volume Proceedings of the Demo and Poster Sessions*. Association for Computational Linguistics, Prague, Czech Republic, pages 177–180. http://www.aclweb.org/anthology/P/P07/P07-2045.

Lemao Liu, Masao Utiyama, Andrew Finch, and Eiichiro Sumita. 2016. Neural machine translation with supervised attention. In *Proceedings of COLING 2016, the 26th International Conference on Computational Linguistics: Technical Papers*. The COLING 2016 Organizing Committee, Osaka, Japan, pages 3093–3102. http://aclweb.org/anthology/C16-1291.

Minh-Thang Luong and Christopher D Manning. 2015. Stanford neural machine translation systems for spoken language domains. In *Proceedings of the International Workshop on Spoken Language Translation*.

Thang Luong, Ilya Sutskever, Quoc Le, Oriol Vinyals, and Wojciech Zaremba. 2015. Addressing the rare word problem in neural machine translation. In *Proceedings of the 53rd Annual Meeting of the Association for Computational Linguistics and the 7th International Joint Conference on Natural Language Processing (Volume 1: Long Papers)*. Association for Computational Linguistics, Beijing, China, pages 11–19. http://www.aclweb.org/anthology/P15-1002.

Jean Pouget-Abadie, Dzmitry Bahdanau, Bart van Merrienboer, KyungHyun Cho, and Yoshua Bengio. 2014. Overcoming the curse of sentence length for neural machine translation using automatic segmentation. *CoRR* abs/1409.1257. http://arxiv.org/abs/1409.1257.

Rico Sennrich, Orhan Firat, Kyunghyun Cho, Alexandra Birch, Barry Haddow, Julian Hitschler, Marcin Junczys-Dowmunt, Samuel Läubli, Antonio Valerio Miceli Barone, Jozef Mokry, and Maria Nadejde. 2017. Nematus: a toolkit for neural machine translation. In *Proceedings of the Software Demonstrations of the 15th Conference of the European Chapter of the Association for Computational Linguistics*. Association for Computational Linguistics, Valencia, Spain, pages 65–68. http://aclweb.org/anthology/E17-3017.

Rico Sennrich, Barry Haddow, and Alexandra Birch. 2016a. Edinburgh neural machine translation systems for WMT 16. In *Proceedings of the First Conference on Machine Translation (WMT)*. Association for Computational Linguistics, Berlin, Germany, pages 371–376.

http://www.aclweb.org/anthology/W/W16/W16-2323.

Rico Sennrich, Barry Haddow, and Alexandra Birch. 2016b. Neural machine translation of rare words with subword units. In *Proceedings of the 54th Annual Meeting of the Association for Computational Linguistics (Volume 1: Long Papers)*. Association for Computational Linguistics, Berlin, Germany, pages 1715–1725. http://www.aclweb.org/anthology/P16-1162.

Jörg Tiedemann. 2012. Parallel data, tools and interfaces in opus. In Nicoletta Calzolari (Conference Chair), Khalid Choukri, Thierry Declerck, Mehmet Ugur Dogan, Bente Maegaard, Joseph Mariani, Jan Odijk, and Stelios Piperidis, editors, *Proceedings of the Eight International Conference on Language Resources and Evaluation (LREC'12)*. European Language Resources Association (ELRA), Istanbul, Turkey.

Antonio Toral and Víctor M. Sánchez-Cartagena. 2017. A multifaceted evaluation of neural versus phrase-based machine translation for 9 language directions. In *Proceedings of the 15th Conference of the European Chapter of the Association for Computational Linguistics: Volume 1, Long Papers*. Association for Computational Linguistics, Valencia, Spain, pages 1063–1073. http://www.aclweb.org/anthology/E17-1100.

Zhaopeng Tu, Zhengdong Lu, Yang Liu, Xiaohua Liu, and Hang Li. 2016. Modeling coverage for neural machine translation. In *Proceedings of the 54th Annual Meeting of the Association for Computational Linguistics (Volume 1: Long Papers)*. Association for Computational Linguistics, Berlin, Germany, pages 76–85. http://www.aclweb.org/anthology/P16-1008.

Marco Turchi, Tijl De Bie, and Nello Cristianini. 2008. Learning performance of a machine translation system: a statistical and computational analysis. In *Proceedings of the Third Workshop on Statistical Machine Translation*. Association for Computational Linguistics, Columbus, Ohio, pages 35–43. http://www.aclweb.org/anthology/W/W08/W08-0305.

Philip Williams, Rico Sennrich, Maria Nadejde, Matthias Huck, Barry Haddow, and Ondřej Bojar. 2016. Edinburgh's statistical machine translation systems for wmt16. In *Proceedings of the First Conference on Machine Translation*. Association for Computational Linguistics, Berlin, Germany, pages 399–410. http://www.aclweb.org/anthology/W/W16/W16-2327.

Yonghui Wu, Mike Schuster, Zhifeng Chen, Quoc V. Le, Mohammad Norouzi, Wolfgang Macherey, Maxim Krikun, Yuan Cao, Qin Gao, Klaus Macherey, Jeff Klingner, Apurva Shah, Melvin Johnson, Xiaobing Liu, Lukasz Kaiser, Stephan Gouws, Yoshikiyo Kato, Taku Kudo, Hideto Kazawa, Keith Stevens, George Kurian, Nishant Patil, Wei Wang, Cliff Young, Jason Smith, Jason Riesa, Alex Rudnick, Oriol Vinyals, Greg Corrado, Macduff Hughes, and Jeffrey Dean. 2016. Google's neural machine translation system: Bridging the gap between human and machine translation. *CoRR* abs/1609.08144. http://arxiv.org/abs/1609.08144.pdf.

# Cost Weighting for Neural Machine Translation Domain Adaptation

**Boxing Chen, Colin Cherry, George Foster, and Samuel Larkin**
National Research Council Canada
Ottawa, ON, Canada
`First.Last@nrc-cnrc.gc.ca`

## Abstract

In this paper, we propose a new domain adaptation technique for neural machine translation called cost weighting, which is appropriate for adaptation scenarios in which a small in-domain data set and a large general-domain data set are available. Cost weighting incorporates a domain classifier into the neural machine translation training algorithm, using features derived from the encoder representation in order to distinguish in-domain from out-of-domain data. Classifier probabilities are used to weight sentences according to their domain similarity when updating the parameters of the neural translation model. We compare cost weighting to two traditional domain adaptation techniques developed for statistical machine translation: data selection and sub-corpus weighting. Experiments on two large-data tasks show that both the traditional techniques and our novel proposal lead to significant gains, with cost weighting outperforming the traditional methods.

## 1   Introduction

The performance of data-driven machine translation techniques depends heavily on the degree of domain match between training and test data, where "domain" indicates a particular combination of factors such as genre, topic, national origin, dialect, or author's or publication's style (Chen et al., 2013). Training data varies significantly across domains, and cross-domain translations are unreliable, so performance can often be improved by adapting the MT system to the test domain.

Domain adaptation (DA) techniques for SMT systems have been widely studied. Approaches include self-training, data selection, data weighting, context-based DA, and topic-based DA, etc. We review these techniques in the next section.

Sequence-to-sequence learning (Bahdanau et al., 2015; Sutskever et al., 2015) has achieved great success on machine translation tasks recently (Sennrich et al., 2016a), and is often referred to as Neural Machine Translation (NMT). NMT usually adopts the encoder-decoder framework: it first encodes a source sentence into context vector(s), then decodes its translation token-by-token, selecting from the target vocabulary. Attention based NMT (Bahdanau et al., 2015; Luong et al., 2015) dynamically generates context vectors for each target position, and focuses on the relevant source words when generating a target word.

Domain adaptation for NMT is still a new research area, with only a small number of relevant publications. Luong et al. (2015) adapted an NMT model trained on general domain data with further training (*fine-tuning*) on in-domain data only. This was called the *continue* model by (Freitag and Al-Onaizan, 2016), who propose an ensemble method that combines the continue model with the original model. Chu et al. (2017) propose a method called *mixed fine tuning*, which combines fine tuning and multi domain NMT.

In this paper, we propose a new domain adaptation method for NMT called cost weighting, in which a domain classifier and sequence-to-sequence translation model are trained simultaneously. The domain classifier is trained on in-domain and general domain data, and provides an estimate of the probability that each sentence in the training data is in-domain. The cost incurred for each sentence is weighted by the probability of it being in-domain. This biases the sequence-to-sequence model toward in-domain data, resulting in improved translation performance on an in-domain test set.



*Proceedings of the First Workshop on Neural Machine Translation*, pages 40–46,
Vancouver, Canada, August 4, 2017. ©2017 Association for Computational Linguistics

We also study the application of existing SMT domain adaptation techniques to NMT, specifically data selection and corpus weighting methods.

Experiments on Chinese-to-English NIST and English-to-French WMT tasks show that: 1) data selection and corpus weighting methods yield significant improvement over the non-adapted baseline; and 2) the new cost weighting method obtains the biggest improvement. The cost weighting scheme has the additional advantage of being integrated with sequence-to-sequence training.

## 2 Applying SMT adaptation techniques to NMT

There are several adaptation scenarios for MT, of which the most common is: 1) the training material is heterogeneous, with some parts that are not too far from the test domain; 2) a bilingual development set drawn from the test domain is available. In this paper, we study adaptation techniques for this scenario.

### 2.1 SMT adaptation techniques

Most SMT domain adaptation (DA) techniques can be classified into one of five categories: self-training, context-based DA, topic-based DA, data selection, and data weighting.

With self-training (Ueffing and Ney, 2007; Schwenk, 2008; Bertoldi and Federico, 2009), an MT system trained on general domain data is used to translate large in-domain monolingual data. The resulting bilingual sentence pairs are then used as additional training data. Sennrich (2016b) has shown that back-translating a large amount of target-language text and using the resulting synthetic parallel text can improve NMT performance significantly. We can expect greater improvement if the monolingual data are in-domain. This method assumes the availability of large amounts of in-domain monolingual data, which is not the adaptation scenario in this paper.

Context-based DA includes word sense disambiguation for adaptation (Carpuat et al., 2013), which employs local context to distinguish the translations for different domains. The cache-based method (Tiedemann, 2010; Gong et al., 2011) uses local or document-level context.

Work on topic-based DA includes (Tam et al., 2007; Eidelman et al., 2012; Hasler et al., 2012; Hewavitharana et al., 2013), and employs a topic model to distinguish the translations for different topics.

Data selection approaches (Moore and Lewis, 2010; Axelrod et al., 2011; Duh et al., 2013; Chen and Huang, 2016) search for data that are similar to the in-domain data according to some criterion, then use the results for training, either alone or in combination with existing data.

Data weighting approaches weight each data item according to its proximity to the in-domain data. This can be applied at corpus (Foster and Kuhn, 2007; Sennrich, 2012), sentence (Matsoukas et al., 2009), or phrase level (Foster et al., 2010; Chen et al., 2013).

### 2.2 Application to NMT

In this paper, we apply data selection, corpus weighting, and sentence weighting strategies to NMT.

**Data selection** Some previous work (Luong and Manning, 2015; Sennrich et al., 2016b) has shown that the performance of NMT systems is highly sensitive to data size. Therefore, we follow the solution in (Luong and Manning, 2015): we first train an NMT system on all available training data, then further train on the selected in-domain data. We adopt two data selection methods in this paper. The first one is based on bilingual language model cross-entropy difference (Axelrod et al., 2011). For both the source and target language, two language models are trained on in-domain and out-of-domain data respectively; then, a sentence pair is evaluated with the cross-entropy difference according to the language models. The second method is semi-supervised convolutional neural network based data selection (Chen and Huang, 2016). The in-domain data and randomly sampled general-domain data are used to train a domain classifier with semi-supervised CNN, then this classifier computes domain relevance scores for all the sentences in the general-domain data set.

**Sub-corpus weighting** To weight different sub-corpora, we first train NMT sub-models on them, then combine these in a weighted fashion. Specifically, we: 1) train an NMT model on the large combined general-domain corpus; 2) initialize with the previous model, and train several new models on sub-corpora; 3) weight each sub-corpus according to its proximity to the in-domain data (dev set), using target-side language model perplexity (Foster and Kuhn, 2007; Sennrich, 2012); and 4) take a weighted average of the parameters in the sub-models to form our final adapted model. **Sentence-level weighting** Our new method for weighting individual sentence pairs uses a classifier to assign weights, and applies them when computing the cost of each mini-batch during NMT training. We defer a detailed description to section 4, after first presenting the NMT approach used in our experiments.

## 3  Neural machine translation

Attention-based neural machine translation systems (Bahdanau et al., 2014) are typically implemented with a recurrent neural network (RNN) based encoder-decoder framework. Suppose we have a source sentence $x = x_1, x_2, ..., x_m$ and its translation $y = y_1, y_2, ..., y_n$. The probability of the target sentence $y$ given a source sentence $x$ is modeled as follows:

$$p(y|x) = \prod_{t=1}^{n} p(y_t|y_{<t}, x),  \quad (1)$$

where $y_{<t}$ stands for all previous translated words.

The NMT encoder reads the source sentence $x$ and encodes it into a sequence of hidden states $h = h_1, h_2, ..., h_m$. Each hidden state $h_i$ is computed from the previous hidden state $h_{i-1}$ and the current source word $x_i$, using a recurrent unit such as Long Short-Term Memory (LSTM) (Sutskever et al., 2014) or Gated Recurrent Unit (GRU) (Bahdanau et al., 2014).

$$\overrightarrow{h}_i = f(\overrightarrow{h}_{i-1}, x_i)  \quad (2)$$

As is standard practice, we use the concatenation of the forward hidden state $\overrightarrow{h}_i$ and backward hidden state $\overleftarrow{h}_i$ for the source word $x_i$ to form an aggregated state $h_i$.

The decoder is a recurrent neural network that predicts the next word in the target sequence. The conditional probability of each word $y_t$ is computed with its previously generated words $y_{<t}$, a recurrent hidden state $s_t$, and a *context vector* $c_t$:

$$p(y_t|y_{<t}, x) = g(y_t, s_t, c_t)  \quad (3)$$

The context vector $c_t$ is introduced to capture the relevant part of the source sentence, which is computed as a weighted sum of the annotations $h_i$. The weight of each annotation $h_i$ is computed through an alignment model $\alpha_{ti}$, which is a feed-forward neural network to model the probability that $y_t$ is aligned to $x_i$.

$$c_t = \sum_{i=1}^{m} \alpha_{ti} h_i,  \quad (4)$$

where the $\alpha_{ti}$ are normalized outputs from a softmax operation.

The hidden state $s_t$ is the decoder RNN hidden state at time $t$, computed by a recurrent unit such as an LSTM or GRU.

$$s_t = q(s_{t-1}, y_{t-1}, c_t)  \quad (5)$$

In the above equations, $f, g, q$ are all non-linear functions.

Given a bilingual corpus $D$, the parameters in the neural network $\theta$ are learned by maximizing the (potentially regularized) conditional log-likelihood:

$$\theta^\star = \arg\max_{\theta} \sum_{(x,y)\in D} \log p(y|x; \theta)  \quad (6)$$

## 4  Cost weighting based adaptation

The data selection and corpus-weighting approaches described above involve fine-tuning one or more NMT systems on data subsets, where data selection fine-tunes on subsets that are selected according to similarity to the development set, and sub-corpus weighting fine-tunes on predetermined subsets, with the fine-tuned models being combined according to the subsets' similarity to the development set.

Our cost weighting scheme for neural machine translation departs from these strategies in two ways. First of all, we do not adopt a fine-tuning strategy, but instead directly scale the NMT system's top-level costs according to each training sentence's similarity to the development set. Second, development set similarity is determined by a feed-forward neural network, which is learned alongside the NMT parameters, and which uses the highly informative NMT source encoder to provide its input representation.

### 4.1  Classifier

At the core of our method is a probabilistic, binary classifier that attempts to determine whether or not a source sentence was drawn from our development set. Once trained, we expect this classifier to assign high probabilities to sentences that are similar to our development set, and low probability to others. This classifier first uses an attention-like aggregator to transform the encoder hidden states $h_i$ into a fixed-length vector representation $r_x$:

$$r_x = \sum_{i=1}^{m} \beta_i h_i$$

$$\text{where } \beta_i = \frac{\exp(\gamma_i)}{\sum_i^m \exp(\gamma_i)}$$

$$\text{and } \gamma_i = \tanh(W^\beta h_i + b^\beta)^\top w^\beta$$

We then pass the source representation vector $r_x$ into a two-layer perceptron whose top-level activation is a sigmoid, allowing us to interpret its final score as a probability.

$$p_d(x) = \sigma\left(\tanh\left(W^d r_x + b^d\right)^\top w^d\right)$$

$$\text{where } \sigma(x) = \frac{1}{1 + \exp(-x)}$$

We train this classifier with a cross entropy loss, maximizing $p_d(x)$ for source sentences drawn from the development set, and minimizing it for those drawn from the training set. Each classifier minibatch is populated with an equal number of training and development sentences, randomly drawn from their respective sets. Crucially, we do not back-propagate the classifier loss to the encoder parameters. The classifier is trained by updating only $W^\beta$, $w^\beta$, $b^\beta$, $W^d$, $w^d$ and $b^d$, treating the sequence $h_i, i = 1 \ldots m$ as an informative, but constant, representation of its input $x$.

### 4.2 Weighted Costs

With our source-sentence domain classifier $p_d(x)$ in place, it is straight-forward to use it to scale our costs to emphasize training sentences that are similar to our development set. Scaling costs with a multiplicative scalar is similar to adjusting the learning rate: it changes the magnitude of the parameter update without changing its direction. We alter equation 6 as follows:

$$\theta^\star = \arg\max_\theta \sum_{(x,y)\in D} (1 + p_d(x)) \log p(y|x; \theta)$$

$$(7)$$

Note that we scale our log NMT cost by 1 plus our domain probability $p_d(x)$. We do this because these probabilities tend to be very low: the classifier is able to correctly determine that training sentences are not in fact development sentences. By adding 1 to this probability, very low-probability sentences are updated as normal, while high-probability sentences are given a bonus. For the purposes of NMT training $p_d(x)$ is treated as a constant; that is, the NMT loss does not back-propagate to the classifier parameters.

### 4.3 Implementation Details

Starting from random parameters for both models, we alternate between optimizing the weighted NMT objective in Equation 7, and the classifier's cross-entropy objective. Training the two concurrently allows the classifier to benefit from and adjust to improvements in the encoder representation. Meanwhile, the NMT objective becomes increasingly focused on in-domain sentences as the classifier improves. We perform one NMT minibatch of size $b$, and then a classifier minibatch of size $2b$ ($b$ training sentences and $b$ development sentences). Training sentences for NMT and classifier updates are sampled independently. Note that classifier updates are much faster than NMT updates, as the classifier makes only one binary decision per sentence.

We have also experimented with versions of the system where we train an unweighted NMT system first, and use it to initialize training with weighted costs, similar to fine tuning. This works as well as using costs throughout, and has the speed benefits that come from starting with an initialized NMT model. However, all of the cost weighting results reported in this paper come from systems that use costs throughout training.

## 5 Experiments

### 5.1 Data

We conducted experiments on two translation tasks. The first one is the Chinese-to-English NIST task. We used NIST06 and NIST08 test sets as the dev set and test set, which contain 1,664 and 1,357 source sentences respectively and each source sentence has 4 target references. Their domain is the combination of newswire and weblog genre. The training data are from LDC; we manually selected about 1.7 million sentence pairs, composed of various sub-domains, such as newswire, weblog, webforum, short message, etc. The second task is the English-to-French WMT task.[1] The dev set is a concatenation of new-stest2012 and 2013 test sets, which contains 6,003 sentence pairs; the test set is newstest2014, which contains 3,003 sentence pairs. The training data contain 12 million sentence pairs, composed of various sub-domains, such as news commentary, Europarl, UN, common crawl web data, etc. In the corpus weighting adaptation experiment, we manually grouped the data into 4 sub-corpora according to provenance for both tasks.

### 5.2 Setting

The NMT system we used is based on the open source Nematus toolkit (Sennrich et al., 2016b).[2] We segmented words via byte-pair encoding on both the source and target side of the training data (Sennrich et al., 2016b). The source and target vocabulary sizes of the Chinese-to-English system were both 60K, and those of the English-to-French system were 90K. The source word embedding dimension size was 512, and the target word embedding dimension size was 1024. The mini-batch size was 100, and the maximum sequence length was 50. We used the Adadelta optimization algorithm to train the system. Our domain classifier described in Section 4.1 has a hidden-layer size of 1024. Its attention-like aggregator also uses a hidden-layer size of 1024. The classifier is also optimized with Adadelta.

In the data selection experiments, we followed (Chen and Huang, 2016) to set all parameters for the cross-entropy difference and semi-supervised CNN based data selection. For language model based selection, we used 3-gram LMs with Witten-Bell[3] smoothing. For Semi-supervised CNN based data selection, we generate one-hot and word-embedding-based bag-of-word regions and n-gram regions and input them to the CNN. We set the region size to 5 and stride size to 1. The non-linear function we chose is "ReLU", the number of weight vectors or neurons is 500. We use the online available CNN toolkit $conText$[4]. To train the general domain word embedding, we used $word2vec$[5]. The size of the vector was set to 300. We select the top 10% of the sentence pairs

---

[1]The data is available at http://www-lium.univ-lemans.fr/ schwenk/nnmt-shared-task/

[2]https://github.com/rsennrich/nematus

[3]For small amounts of data, Witten-Bell smoothing performed better than Kneser-Ney smoothing in our experiments

[4]http://riejohnson.com/cnn_download.html

[5]https://code.google.com/archive/p/word2vec/

|              | zh2en  | $\Delta$ | en2fr | $\Delta$ |
|--------------|--------|----------|-------|----------|
| baseline     | 32.9   | –        | 35.8  | –        |
| avg weighting| 33.1   | 0.2      | 36.1  | 0.3      |
| crp weighting| 33.5*  | 0.6      | 36.3* | 0.5      |
| DS xent      | 33.5*  | 0.6      | 36.3* | 0.5      |
| DS sscnn     | 33.8** | 0.9      | 36.4* | 0.6      |
| cost weighting| 34.1**| 1.2      | 36.6**| 0.8      |

Table 1: BLEU scores for ensembled baseline and domain adapted systems, which include average weighting ("avg weighting"), corpus weighting ("crp weighting") ensemble, ensembled cross-entropy based data selection ("DS xent"), semi-supervised CNN based data selection ("DS sscnn"), and cost weighting based systems. */** means the result is significantly better than the baseline at $p < 0.05$ or $p < 0.01$ level, respectively.

from the whole training data to fine-tune the NMT system.

### 5.3 Results

We evaluated the system using BLEU score (Papineni et al., 2002) on the test set. Following (Koehn, 2004), we use bootstrap resampling for significance testing. As shown in (Sennrich et al., 2016b), simply averaging the models from several checkpoints can improve NMT translation performance. Because the data selection and corpus weighting methods applied fine-tuning, for a fair comparison, all of our systems applied a two-pass training strategy. That is, we train the system using algorithm Adadelta until it is converged or early stopped, then resume the training using algorithm RMSProp (Hinton et al., 2012). Moreover, because the corpus weighting method combines 4 models fine-tuned on different sub-corpora, for a fair comparison all of our systems are ensemble systems which average the models from the 4 checkpoints with highest BLEU scores on the dev set. Table 1 summarizes the results for both tasks.

Both tasks are challenging to improve with domain adaptation techniques, because the training data for the baselines in both have already been selected to a certain extent. However, we still obtained statistically significant improvements using the adaptation techniques developed for SMT. This demonstrates the usefulness of existing adaptation techniques. More importantly, we obtained larger and more significant improvement from the cost weighting technique.

### 5.4 Discussion

All three domain adaptation techniques evaluated in this paper share a similar idea, namely when training the system, rely more on those training samples which are closer to the in-domain data. The techniques differ in granularity: corpus weighting operates on the sub-corpus level, while data selection and cost weighting operate on the sentence level. They also differ in weighting latency: data selection and corpus weighting measure domain proximity only once prior to system training, while cost weighting repeatedly updates its proximity estimates as the system is trained. Finally, they differ in proximity metrics: data selection and corpus weighting measure domain similarity with external criteria such as LM cross-entropy or CNN sentence representations, while cost weighting uses RNN representations shared with the sequence-to-sequence model. Also, cost weighting applies its sentence weights directly to the training process, instead of thresholding the weights to select sentences.

## 6 Conclusions

In this paper, we have successfully applied the SMT domain adaptation techniques, data selection and corpus weighting, to neural machine translation (NMT). We also proposed a new cost weighting technique for neural machine translation domain adaptation. This method trains the classifier and sequence-to-sequence translation model simultaneously; in-domain proximity values are computed on the fly with the sequence-to-sequence model, which is more precise and also makes online adaptation possible. Experiments on the Chinese-English NIST task and the English-French WMT task showed that both existing techniques and the novel cost weighting technique all improve performance over the baseline, with the cost weighting method obtaining the best improvement.

## 7 Future Work

We would like to devise experiments to better understand whether the improvements we are seeing in domain adaptation are from our adaptive domain classifier, or from applying the classifier outputs as cost weights. For example, we could test cost weighting with fixed weights from the CNN domain classifier of Chen and Huang (2016), and see if that results in similar improvements.

We would also like to explore invariant weighted updates (Karampatziakis and Langford, 2010), which maintain the invariance property that updating the model with importance weight $2p$ is equivalent to updating twice with weight $p$. Invariant updates have been shown to perform better than simply scaling the cost or learning rate as we do here, but previous work has all been in the context of linear models.


## References

Amittai Axelrod, Xiaodong He, and Jianfeng Gao. 2011. Domain adaptation via pseudo in-domain data selection. In *EMNLP 2011*.

Dzmitry Bahdanau, Kyunghyun Cho, and Yoshua Bengio. 2014. Neural machine translation by jointly learning to align and translate. *CoRR*, abs/1409.0473.

Nicola Bertoldi and Marcello Federico. 2009. Domain adaptation for statistical machine translation with monolingual resources. In *Proceedings of the 4th Workshop on Statistical Machine Translation*, Athens, March. WMT.

Marine Carpuat, Hal Daume III, Katharine Henry, Ann Irvine, Jagadeesh Jagarlamudi, and Rachel Rudinger. 2013. Sensespotting: Never let your parallel data tie you to an old domain. In *Proceedings of the 51st Annual Meeting of the Association for Computational Linguistics (Volume 1: Long Papers)*, pages 1435–1445, Sofia, Bulgaria, August.

Boxing Chen and Fei Huang. 2016. Semi-supervised convolutional networks for translation adaptation with tiny amount of in-domain data. In *Proceedings of the 20th SIGNLL Conference on Computational Natural Language Learning, CoNLL 2016, Berlin, Germany, August 11-12, 2016*, pages 314–323.

Boxing Chen, Roland Kuhn, and George Foster. 2013. Vector space model for adaptation in statistical machine translation. In *Proceedings of the 51st Annual Meeting of the Association for Computational Linguistics (Volume 1: Long Papers)*, pages 1285–1293, Sofia, Bulgaria, August.

Chenhui Chu, Raj Dabre, and Sadao Kurohashi. 2017. An empirical comparison of simple domain adaptation methods for neural machine translation. *CoRR*, abs/1701.03214.

Kevin Duh, Graham Neubig, Katsuhito Sudoh, and Hajime Tsukada. 2013. Adaptation data selection using neural language models: Experiments in machine translation. In *Proceedings of the 51st Annual Meeting of the Association for Computational Linguistics (Volume 2: Short Papers)*, pages 678–683, Sofia, Bulgaria, August.

Vladimir Eidelman, Jordan Boyd-Graber, and Philip Resnik. 2012. Topic models for dynamic translation model adaptation. In *Proceedings of the 50th Annual Meeting of the Association for Computational Linguistics (Volume 2: Short Papers)*, pages 115–119, Jeju Island, Korea, July.

George Foster and Roland Kuhn. 2007. Mixture-model adaptation for SMT. In *Proceedings of the ACL Workshop on Statistical Machine Translation*, Prague, June. WMT.

George Foster, Cyril Goutte, and Roland Kuhn. 2010. Discriminative instance weighting for domain adaptation in statistical machine translation. In *Proceedings of the 2010 Conference on Empirical Methods in Natural Language Processing (EMNLP)*, Boston.

Markus Freitag and Yaser Al-Onaizan. 2016. Fast domain adaptation for neural machine translation. *CoRR*, abs/1612.06897.

Z. Gong, M. Zhang, and G. Zhou. 2011. Cache-based document-level statistical machine translation. In *EMNLP 2011*.

Eva Hasler, Barry Haddow, and Philipp Koehn. 2012. Sparse lexicalised features and topic adaptation for smt. In *Proceedings of IWSLT*, Hongkong.

Sanjika Hewavitharana, Dennis Mehay, Sankaranarayanan Ananthakrishnan, and Prem Natarajan. 2013. Incremental topic-based translation model adaptation for conversational spoken language translation. In *Proceedings of the 51st Annual Meeting of the Association for Computational Linguistics (Volume 2: Short Papers)*, pages 697–701, Sofia, Bulgaria, August.

Geoffrey Hinton, N Srivastava, and Kevin Swersky. 2012. Lecture 6a overview of minibatch gradient descent. In *Coursera Lecture slides*.

Nikos Karampatziakis and John Langford. 2010. Importance weight aware gradient updates. *CoRR*, abs/1011.1576.

Philipp Koehn. 2004. Statistical significance tests for machine translation evaluation. In *Proceedings of the 2004 Conference on Empirical Methods in Natural Language Processing (EMNLP)*, Barcelona, Spain.

Minh-Thang Luong and Christopher D. Manning. 2015. Stanford neural machine translation systems for spoken language domain. In *International Workshop on Spoken Language Translation*, Da Nang, Vietnam.

Spyros Matsoukas, Antti-Veikko I. Rosti, and Bing Zhang. 2009. Discriminative corpus weight estimation for machine translation. In *Proceedings of the 2009 Conference on Empirical Methods in Natural Language Processing (EMNLP)*, Singapore.

Robert C. Moore and William Lewis. 2010. Intelligent selection of language model training data. In *ACL 2010*.

Kishore Papineni, Salim Roukos, Todd Ward, and Wei-Jing Zhu. 2002. BLEU: A method for automatic evaluation of Machine Translation. In *Proceedings of the 40th Annual Meeting of the Association for Computational Linguistics (ACL)*, pages 311–318, Philadelphia, July. ACL.

Holger Schwenk. 2008. Investigations on large-scale lightly-supervised training for statistical machine translation. In *IWSLT 2008*.

Rico Sennrich, Barry Haddow, and Alexandra Birch. 2016a. Edinburgh Neural machine translation systems for WMT 16. In *Proceedings of the First Conference on Machine Translation (WMT2016)*, Berlin, Germany.

Rico Sennrich, Barry Haddow, and Alexandra Birch. 2016b. Improving neural machine translation models with monolingual data. In *Proceedings of the 54th Annual Meeting of the Association for Computational Linguistics (Volume 1: Long Papers)*, pages 86–96, Berlin, Germany, August. Association for Computational Linguistics.

Rico Sennrich. 2012. Perplexity minimization for translation model domain adaptation in statistical machine translation. In *EACL 2012*.

Ilya Sutskever, Oriol Vinyals, and Quoc V. Le. 2014. Sequence to sequence learning with neural networks. *CoRR*, abs/1409.3215.

Yik-Cheung Tam, Ian Lane, and Tanja Schultz. 2007. Bilingual-LSA Based LM Adaptation for Spoken Language Translation. In *Proceedings of the 45th Annual Meeting of the Association for Computational Linguistics (ACL)*, Prague, Czech Republic, June. ACL.

Jg Tiedemann. 2010. Context adaptation in statistical machine translation using models with exponentially decaying cache. In *DANLP*.

Nicola Ueffing and Hermann Ney. 2007. Word-level confidence estimation for machine translation. *Computational Linguistics*, 33(1):9–40.

# Detecting Untranslated Content for Neural Machine Translation


**Isao Goto**  **Hideki Tanaka**

NHK Science & Technology Research Laboratories,
1-10-11 Kinuta, Setagaya-ku,
Tokyo 157-8510, Japan

`goto.i-es@nhk.or.jp`    `tanaka.h-ja@nhk.or.jp`



## Abstract

Despite its promise, neural machine translation (NMT) has a serious problem in that source content may be mistakenly left untranslated. The ability to detect untranslated content is important for the practical use of NMT. We evaluate two types of probability with which to detect untranslated content: the cumulative attention (ATN) probability and back translation (BT) probability from the target sentence to the source sentence. Experiments on detecting untranslated content in Japanese–English patent translations show that ATN and BT are each more effective than random choice, BT is more effective than ATN, and the combination of the two provides further improvements. We also confirmed the effectiveness of using ATN and BT to rerank the $n$-best NMT outputs.


## 1 Introduction

Neural machine translation (NMT) (Sutskever et al., 2014; Bahdanau et al., 2015) outputs fluent translations. However, some of the source content—not only word-level expressions but also clause-level expressions—is sometimes missing from the output translation, especially when NMT translates long sentences. An example is shown in Figure 1. The occurrence of untranslated content is a serious problem limiting practical use of NMT.

Conventional statistical machine translation (SMT) (Koehn et al., 2003; Chiang, 2007) explicitly distinguishes the untranslated source words from the translated source words in decoding and keeps translating until no untranslated source words remain. However, NMT does not explicitly distinguish untranslated words from translated words. This means NMT cannot use coverage vectors as are used in SMT to prevent translations from being dropped.

There are methods that use dynamic states, which are regarded as a soft coverage vector, at each source word position (Tu et al., 2016b; Mi et al., 2016). These methods will alleviate the problem; however, they do not decide whether to terminate decoding on the basis of the detection of untranslated content. Therefore, the translation dropping problem remains.

We evaluated two types of probability for detecting untranslated content. One type is the cumulative attention (ATN) probability for each source position. The other type is the back translation (BT) probability of each source word from the MT output. The latter type does not necessarily require word-level correspondences between languages, which are not easy to infer precisely in NMT. We also compared direct use of the probabilities and the use of the ratio of the probabilities, which compares the negative logarithm of a probability to the minimum value of the negative logarithm of the probability in the $n$-best outputs. In addition, we evaluated the effect of using detection scores to rerank the $n$-best outputs of NMT.

We conducted experiments for the detection of untranslated source content words in 100 sentences with MT outputs translated using NMT on Japanese–English patent translation task data sets. The results are as follows. The detection accuracies achieved using the ratio of probabilities were higher than those achieved directly using the probabilities. ATN and BT are each more effective than random choice at detecting untranslated content. BT was better than ATN. The detection accuracy further improved when ATN and BT were used together. Reranking using the scores of the two types of probabilities improved the BLEU scores. BLEU scores improved further when the detection

47


*Proceedings of the First Workshop on Neural Machine Translation*, pages 47–55,
Vancouver, Canada, August 4, 2017. ©2017 Association for Computational Linguistics

| Input | その後、 第1段から順に第M段まで 、ADC＃1とADC＃2のパイプラインゲインエラー補<br>正を交互に繰り返す（ステップS6とS7、ステップS8と S9、ステップS10と S11）。 |
|---|---|
| Reference | After that , the correction of a pipeline gain error of ADC # 1 and ADC # 2 is sequentially repeated alternately from the first stage to the Mth stage ( steps S6 and S7 , steps S8 and S9 , steps S10 and S11 ) . |
| Output | After that , the pipeline gain error correction of the ADC # 1 and the ADC # 2 is alternately repeated ( steps S6 and S7 , steps S8 and S11 ) . |

Figure 1: Example of untranslated content in Japanese–English translation by NMT. The shaded parts in the input were mistakenly not translated. The shaded parts in the reference are the corresponding translations of the untranslated parts.

scores of the two types of probabilities were used together. We counted the number of untranslated content words in 100 sentences and found that the untranslated content in the reranked outputs was less than that in the baseline NMT outputs.

## 2 Neural Machine Translation

We briefly describe the baseline attention-based NMT based on previous work (Bahdanau et al., 2015) that we used. The NMT consists of an encoder that encodes a source sentence and a decoder that generates a target sentence.

Given an input sentence, we convert each word into a one-hot vector and obtain a one-hot vector sequence $\mathbf{x} = x_1, \ldots, x_{Tx}$. The encoder produces a vector $h_j = [\overrightarrow{h}_j^\top ; \overleftarrow{h}_j^\top]^\top$ for each source word position $j$ using long short-term memory (LSTM) (Hochreiter and Schmidhuber, 1997) and the word embedding matrix $E_x$ for the source language. $\overrightarrow{h}_j = f(\overrightarrow{h}_{j-1}, E_x x_j)$ is the vector output by the forward LSTM, where $f$ is the LSTM function, and $\overleftarrow{h}_j = f(\overleftarrow{h}_{j+1}, E_x x_j)$ is the vector output by the backward LSTM.

The decoder calculates the probability of a translation $\mathbf{y} = y_1, \ldots, y_{Ty}$ given $\mathbf{x}$, where $y_i$ is also a one-hot vector at a target word position $i$. The decoder searches $\hat{\mathbf{y}} = \mathrm{argmax}_{\mathbf{y}}\, p(\mathbf{y}|\mathbf{x})$ to output $\hat{\mathbf{y}}$. The probability is decomposed into the product of the probabilities of each word:

$$p(\mathbf{y}|\mathbf{x}) = \prod_i p(y_i|y_1, \ldots, y_{i-1}, \mathbf{x}). \quad (1)$$

Each conditional probability on the right-hand side is modeled as

$$p(y_i|y_1, \ldots, y_{i-1}, \mathbf{x}) = \mathrm{softmax}(y_i^\top W_t t_i), \quad (2)$$
$$t_i = \mathrm{maxout}(U_s s_i + U_y E_y y_{i-1} + U_c c_i), \quad (3)$$

where $s_i$ is a hidden state of the LSTM, $c_i$ is a context vector, $W_.$ and $U_.$ represent weight matrices, and $E_y$ is the word embedding matrix for the target language. The state $s_i$ is calculated as $s_i = f(s_{i-1}, [c_i^\top ; E_y y_{i-1}^\top]^\top)$, where $f$ is the LSTM function. The context vector $c_i$ is calculated as a weighted sum of $h_j$: $c_i = \sum_j \alpha_{i,j} h_j$, where

$$\alpha_{i,j} = \frac{\exp(e_{i,j})}{\sum_j \exp(e_{i,j})}, \quad (4)$$
$$e_{i,j} = v^\top \tanh(W_s s_{i-1} + W_y E_y y_{i-1}). \quad (5)$$

$v$ is a weight vector.

$\alpha_{i,j}$ represents the attention probability, which can be regarded as a probabilistic correspondence between $y_i$ and $x_j$ to some extent.

## 3 Detection of Untranslated Content

We describe the two types of probabilities and their use in detecting untranslated content.[1]

### 3.1 Cumulative Attention Probability

Heavily attended source words would have been translated, while sparsely attended source words would not have been translated (Tu et al., 2016b). Therefore, the ATN probabilities for each source word position should provide clues to the detection of untranslated content. Using Equation (4), we define an ATN probability score (ATN-P) $a_j$, which represents a score of missing the content of $x_j$ from $\mathbf{y}$, as

$$a_j = -\log\left(\sum_i \alpha_{i,j}\right). \quad (6)$$

The value[2] in parentheses in Equation (6) is the ATN probability at the source position $j$ in $\mathbf{x}$. $i$ represents a target word position in $\mathbf{y}$.

---

[1]The use of their combination is explained in Section 5.2.

[2]Adding a small positive value $\epsilon$ to the value is a practical solution of avoiding calculating $\log(0)$. In our experiments, there was no such case and we did not add $\epsilon$.

However, some source words do not inherently correspond to any target word[3], and one source word may correspond to two or more target words. Therefore, $a_j$ does not always correctly represent the degree of missing the content of $x_j$.

We solve this problem as follows. We define an ATN ratio score (ATN-R), which is based on a probability ratio. Here, the $n$-best outputs are represented as $\mathbf{y}^1, \ldots, \mathbf{y}^n$. Furthermore, we make the following assumption.

**Assumption: Existence of translations**
The translation of an arbitrary input word $x_j, (1 \leq j \leq T_x)$ exists somewhere in the $n$-best outputs $\mathbf{y}^d, (1 \leq d \leq n)$, except when $x_j$ does not inherently correspond to any target words.

Accordingly, we regard $\min_d a_j^d$ as a score without missing a translation, where $a_j^d$ represents $a_j$ for $y^d$. The ATN-R $r_j^d$, which represents a score of dropping the content of $x_j$ from $\mathbf{y}^d$, is defined as

$$r_j^d = a_j^d - \min_{d'}(a_j^{d'}) \qquad (7)$$

This value represents the logarithm of the probability ratio.

### 3.2 Back Translation Probability

We define BT as the forced decoding from an MT output to its input sentence. When the content of a source word is missing in the MT output, the BT probability of the source word is expected to be small. We use this expectation as a clue for detecting untranslated content. A detection method based on the BT probability has the feature that the method does not require the specification of word-level correspondences between languages, which is not easy to infer precisely. Here, we present a BT probability score (BT-P) $b_j^d$ based on the BT probability of $x_j$ from $\mathbf{y}^d$ as

$$b_j^d = -\log(p(x_j|x_1, \ldots, x_{j-1}, \mathbf{y}^d)). \qquad (8)$$

The probability in Equation (8) is calculated using the NMT method described in Section 2.

We again employ the assumption of the "existence of translations" in the previous section and accordingly $\min_d(b_j^d)$ is the score of an output that contains the content of $x_j$. With this, we calculate

a score based on a probability ratio. We define the BT ratio score (BT-R) $q_j^d$, which is a score of missing the content of $x_j$ from $\mathbf{y}^d$, as

$$q_j^d = b_j^d - \min_{d'}(b_j^{d'}). \qquad (9)$$

## 4 Application to Translation Scores

The scores described in the previous section will contribute to the selection of a better output (i.e., one that has less untranslated content) from the $n$-best outputs. We evaluated the effect of reranking using these scores.

As a sentence score for reranking, we use the weighted sum of the output score and the detection score with a weight $\beta$:

$$\log(p(\mathbf{y}^d|\mathbf{x})) - \beta \sum_j r_j^d. \qquad (10)$$

We subtract $r_j^d$, which is a score of missing the content of $x_j$, from the likelihood of the translation. When $q_j^d$ is used, we replace $r_j^d$ with $q_j^d$. Because reranking compares the $n$-best outputs of the same input, the reranking results of ATN-R and those of ATN-P are the same.[4] In the same manner, the reranking results of BT-R and those of BT-P are the same. In what follows, we use ATN-R and BT-R.

When $r_j^d$ and $q_j^d$ are used together, we use the score

$$\log(p(\mathbf{y}^d|\mathbf{x})) - \gamma \sum_j r_j^d - \lambda \sum_j q_j^d, \qquad (11)$$

where $\gamma$ and $\lambda$ are weight parameters.

## 5 Experiments

As translation data sets including long sentences, we chose Japanese–English patent translations. We conducted experiments to confirm the effects of the scores on the detection of untranslated content and the effects on translation.

### 5.1 Common Setup

We used the NTCIR-9 and NTCIR-10 Japanese-to-English translation task data sets (Goto et al., 2011; Goto et al., 2013). The number of parallel sentence pairs in the training data was 3.2M. We

---

[3]For example, articles in English do not usually correspond to any words in Japanese.

[4]However, the results differ when we rank translations among input sentences. The following is an example of such a situation. The translations of many input sentences are ranked and the bottom translations are replaced with the outputs of SMT to reduce missing translation.

used sentences that were 100 words or fewer in length in the training data for Japanese to English (JE) translation. We used sentences that were 50 words or fewer in length in the training data for BT to reduce computational costs. We did not use any monolingual corpus. We used development data consisting of 1000 sentence pairs, which were the first half of the official development data. The numbers of test sentences were 2000 for NTCIR-9 and 2300 for NTCIR-10. We used the Stepp tagger[5] as the English tokenizer and Juman 7.01[6] as the Japanese tokenizer.

We used Kyoto-NMT (Cromieres, 2016) as the NMT implementation and modified it to fit Equation (5). The following settings were used. The most-frequent 30K words were used for both source and target words, and the remaining words were replaced with a special token (UNK). The numbers of LSTM units of the forward and backward encoders were each 1000, the number of LSTM units of the decoder was 1000, the word embedding sizes for the source and target words were each 620, and the size of the vector just before the output layer was 500. The number of hidden layer units and the sizes of the embedding/weight/vocabulary were the same as in (Bahdanau et al., 2015). The mini-batch size for training was 64 for JE and 128 for BT. We used Adam (Kingma and Ba, 2014) to train the NMT models. We trained the NMT models for a total of six epochs. The development data were used to select the best model during the training. The decoding involved a beam search with a beam width of 20. We limited the output length to double the length of the input. We used all of the outputs[7] from the beam search as the $n$-best outputs.[8]

$\beta$, $\gamma$, and $\lambda$ in Section 4 were selected from $\{0.1, 0.2, 0.5, 1, 2\}$ using the development data such that the BLEU score was the highest.

### 5.2 Detecting Untranslated Content

We translated the NTCIR-10 test data from Japanese into English using the baseline NMT system and manually specified untranslated source parts. We then compared the effects of the scores in Section 3 on the detection of untranslated con-

tent.

**Setup**

We prepared the evaluation data as follows. Employing NMT, we translated NTCIR-10 test data whose lengths and reference lengths were each 100 words or fewer.[9] We used the best outputs from the beam search for each test sentence. To pick up translations including untranslated content, we sorted the translations on the basis of (translation length)$/\min$(input length, reference length) in ascending order. We then selected 100 sentences from the top and identified 632 untranslated content words in the 100 selected sentences, which consisted of 4457 words. The 632 identified words were used as the gold data. In this process, we removed the sentences from the selected sentences when we could not identify untranslated parts.

Here, we regarded words including Chinese characters, Arabic numerals, katakana characters, or alphabet letters as content words in Japanese. This is because hiragana characters are basically used for functional roles in Japanese sentences. Even if the part-of-speech is a verb, words comprising only hiragana characters (e.g., *suru*) mainly play formal roles and do not contain substantive meaning in most cases for patents and business documents.

When $r_j^d$ and $q_j^d$ were used together, we calculated the detection score

$$\gamma r_j^d + \lambda q_j^d, \tag{12}$$

where $\gamma$ and $\lambda$ were those selected in Section 5.1.

**Results and Discussion**

We ranked words[10] in the 100 selected source sentences on the basis of the scores described in Section 3 and compared them with the gold data (632 words). The results are shown in Figure 2. The average precision of random choice was $0.14 = 632/4457$. The results were as follows.

- ATN-P and BT-P were more effective than random choice.

- ATN-R was better than ATN-P, and BT-R was better than BT-P for the detection.

- Back translation (BT-R) was more effective than cumulative attention (ATN-R).

---



[5]http://www.nactem.ac.uk/enju/index.html

[6]http://nlp.ist.i.kyoto-u.ac.jp/EN/index.php?JUMAN

[7]Word sequences that were terminated with the end of sentence (EOS) tokens.

[8]$n$ was different for each input. $n$ tended to be large when the input lengths were long.

[9]Sentences longer than 100 words were not included in the training data.

[10]More properly, we ranked word positions.

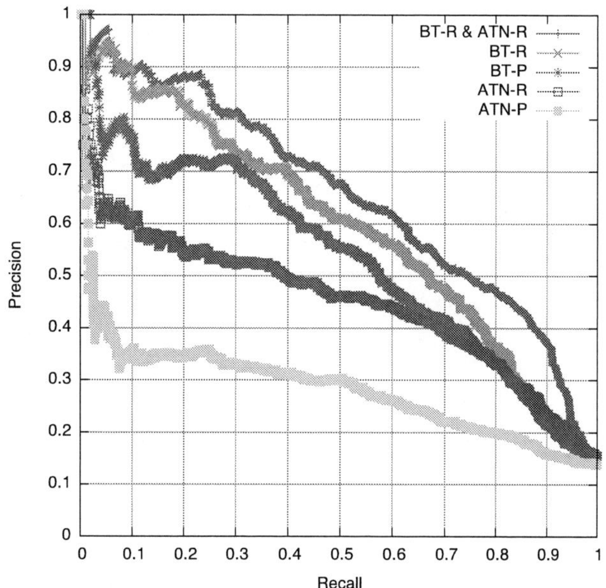

Figure 2: Detection results

| Input | **ISO** 感度 値 が 小さい とき に は 増幅 度 が 小さく 、<br>**ISO** 感度 値 が 大きい とき に は 増幅 度 が 大きい 。 |
|---|---|
| Reference | The amplification is small when the **ISO** sensitivity value is low ,<br>while the amplification is large when the **ISO** sensitivity value is high . |
| Output | When the **ISO** sensitivity value is small , the gain is small . |

Figure 3: Unsuccessful example based on BT. Untranslated parts are shaded.

| Untranslated content | BT-R | ATN-R |
|---|---|---|
| A content word appears only once in an input sentence | Good | Fair |
| A content word appears twice or more in an input sentence | Bad | Fair |

Table 1: Sensitivity of detection of untranslated content.

- The combination of scores (BT-R & ATN-R) was better than the score of each component (BT-R or ATN-R).

Figure 3 shows an unsuccessful example of BT-R. The same content word (ISO) appears twice in the input. It was thus hard to detect the untranslated underlined ISO in the input on the basis of BT-R because the corresponding word (ISO) existed in the output.

On the one hand, the detection sensitivity of BT-P is thought to be high for a content word that appears only once in the input sentence. On the other hand, the detection sensitivity of BT-P is thought to be low for a content word that appears twice or more in the input sentence. Because BT-R is based on BT-P, it has the same characteristics as BT-P. In contrast, ATN-P is sensitive even when a content word appears twice or more in the input sentence because the cumulative probabilities increase depending on the frequency of the word in the MT output. Because ATN-R is based on ATN-P, it has the same characteristics as ATN-P.

Therefore, BT-R and ATN-R are complementary to some extent (Table 1), and this seems to be why the combination works best.

### 5.3 Reranking the $n$-best Outputs

We reranked the $n$-best NMT outputs following Section 4 and assessed the effect on the translation.

### Setup

For comparison, we used the baseline NMT system with soft coverage models (Mi et al., 2016; Tu

|  | NTCIR-10 | NTCIR-9 |
| --- | --- | --- |
| Phrase-based SMT | 30.58 | 30.21 |
| Hierarchical phrase-based SMT | 31.99 | 31.48 |
| NMT Baseline | 38.68 | 37.83 |
| Rerank with ATN-R | 39.82 | 38.88 |
| Rerank with BT-R | 40.14 | 39.16 |
| Rerank with ATN-R & BT-R | 40.36 | 39.46 |
| NMT Baseline with COVERAGE-neural | 38.89 | 37.90 |
| NMT Baseline with COVERAGE-linguistic | 39.13 | 38.03 |

Table 2: Translation results (BLEU)

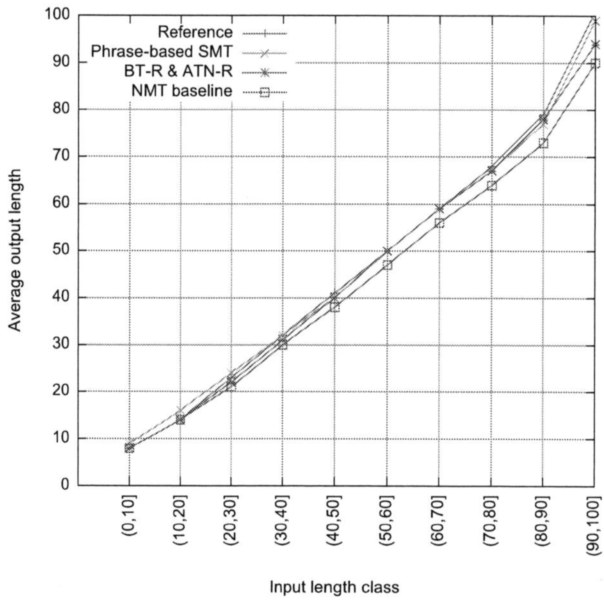


Figure 4: Average output lengths

et al., 2016b), which were used in first-pass decoding.[11] Whereas these studies used gated recurrent units (GRUs) (Chung et al., 2014) for the NMT and coverage models, we used LSTM.[12] The soft coverage model of (Mi et al., 2016) is called a neural soft coverage model (COVERAGE-neural). Tu et al. (2016b) proposed linguistic and neural soft coverage models. We used the linguistic version of (Tu et al., 2016b). We call this model the linguistic soft coverage model (COVERAGE-linguistic).

As references, we used conventional SMT using

Moses (Koehn et al., 2007) with a distortion-limit of 20 for phrase-based SMT and a max-chart-span of 1000 for hierarchical phrase-based SMT.

**Results and Discussion**

Table 2 gives the results measured by case-insensitive BLEU-4 (Papineni et al., 2002). Overall, the results indicate the effectiveness of using ATN probabilities and BT probabilities for translation scores.

We now compare the soft coverage models. Because the difference between the results of the NMT baseline and the results of COVERAGE-neural are small, the effect of COVERAGE-neural was small for this dataset. The difference between the results of the NMT baseline and the results of COVERAGE-linguistic was also small (less than 0.5 BLEU points), whereas the improve-

---

[11]These methods are not competing but are cooperative because they can be used to produce better $n$-best outputs.

[12]Our experiments indicated that the BLEU scores of the baseline NMT system using LSTM were higher than those of the baseline NMT system using GRUs. The training time of the neural soft coverage model using the Chainer (Tokui et al., 2015) LSTM for one epoch was shorter than that of the neural soft coverage model using the Chainer GRU.

|  | Missing translation | Repeated translation |
| --- | --- | --- |
| NMT baseline | 0.061 (137/2251) | 0.004 (9/2251) |
| Rerank with BT-R & ATN-R | 0.020 (45/2251) | 0.004 (9/2251) |

Table 3: Rate of mistakenly untranslated content words (missing translation) and mistakenly repeated translations. The values in parentheses denote the number of source content words.

ment of COVERAGE-linguistic was greater than that of COVERAGE-neural. In contrast, the results of Rerank with ATN-R obtained improvements of more than 1 BLEU point compared with the NMT baseline. Both the soft coverage models and Rerank with ATN-R are based on attention probabilities. The soft coverage models therefore have room for improvement on this dataset, which means that there is a difficulty in training soft coverage models using end-to-end learning to take advantage of the attention probabilities as well as Rerank with ATN-R. The difficulties would depend on the data sets.[13]

We now compare ATN-R and BT-R. ATN-R and BT-R were effective in reranking. BT-R was slightly better than ATN-R. The combined use of ATN-R and BT-R was more effective than using only one component. These results are consistent with the detection results described in Section 5.2. The difference between reranking with BT-R and reranking with ATN-R & BT-R was statistically significant at $\alpha = 0.01$, which was computed using a tool[14] of the bootstrap resampling test (Koehn, 2004).

We compared the average output lengths using NTCIR-10 test data for the test sentences no longer than 100 words. The average output lengths are shown in Figure 4. The figure shows that the average output lengths of the NMT baseline tend to be shorter than the average reference lengths for long sentences. The average lengths of Rerank with BT-R & ATN-R were longer than those of the NMT baseline, and they were closer to the average reference lengths than those of the NMT baseline.

To check whether the amount of untranslated content was reduced by Rerank with ATN-R & BT-R, we counted untranslated content words in 100 randomly selected test sentences from the NTCIR-10 test data and their translations produced by the NMT baseline and by Rerank with ATN-R & BT-R. We removed sentences from the selected test sentences when the test sentence or its reference sentence was longer than 100 words. Words were regarded as content words when the words met the conditions of content words explained in Section 5.2. The results are presented in Table 3. The results confirm that the amount of untranslated content was reduced by Rerank with ATN-R & BT-R without increasing the amount of mistakenly repeated translations.

## 6 Related Work

We introduced soft coverage models (Tu et al., 2016b; Mi et al., 2016) in Section 1. In addition to these published studies, there are several parallel related studies on arXiv (Wu et al., 2016; Li and Jurafsky, 2016; Tu et al., 2016a).[15] Wu et al. (2016) use ATN probabilities for reranking. Li and Jurafsky (2016) use BT probabilities for reranking. Tu et al. (2016a) use probabilities of inputs given the decoder states for reranking. Their probabilities are similar to the BT probabilities that we evaluated. However, unlike BT, to calculate

---

[13] We consider possible reasons that the improvements in the BLEU scores achived with the coverage models were not as great as improvements in (Tu et al., 2016b; Mi et al., 2016) as follows. We compare Figure 4 in this paper and Figure 6 in (Tu et al., 2016b) showing the lengths of translations. Contrary to our baseline results, the output lengths of their baseline were much shorter than those of the phrase-based SMT when source sentences were longer than 50 words. This means that there is less missing content for our baseline than for their baseline. We therefore believe the following reasons explain the smaller improvements achieved with the coverage models.

- There is less room for improvement for our baseline with the coverage models than for their baseline.

- Because there is less missing content for our baseline, there are fewer chances that the coverage model effectively improves the translations in our training, which are necessary to appropriately estimate the coverage model parameters. Therefore, the estimation of the coverage model parameters in our training would be more difficult than that in their training.

The second item is thought to be the reason that the improvements for COVERAGE-linguistic, which has fewer parameters, were larger than those for COVERAGE-neural, which has more parameters.

[14] https://github.com/odashi/mteval

---

[15] Reviewers for EACL 2017 short paper mentioned Li and Jurafsky (2016) and Wu et al. (2016) in their comments. The neural MT tutorial given at NLP 2017 (Annual meeting of the Association for Natural Language Processing in Japan) introduced Tu et al. (2016a).

their probability, the actual $y_i$ selected in the beam search is not used. These studies did not evaluate the effect on detecting untranslated content and did not assess the effect of combining ATN and BT. In contrast, we evaluated the effect on detecting untranslated content for ATN and BT. In addition, we investigated the effect of combining ATN and BT.

## 7 Conclusion

We evaluated the effect of two types of probability on detecting untranslated content, which is a serious problem limiting the practical use of NMT. The two types of probabilities are ATN probabilities and BT probabilities. We confirmed their effectiveness in detecting untranslated content. We also confirmed that they were effective in reranking the $n$-best outputs from NMT. Improvements in NMT will give a better chance of satisfying the assumption of the existence of translations. This is expected to lead to improvements in the detection of untranslated content.

## References


Dzmitry Bahdanau, Kyunghyun Cho, and Yoshua Bengio. 2015. Neural machine translation by jointly learning to align and translate. In *Proceedings of ICLR 2015*.

David Chiang. 2007. Hierarchical phrase-based translation. *Computational Linguistics*, 33(2):201–228.

Junyoung Chung, Çaglar Gülçehre, KyungHyun Cho, and Yoshua Bengio. 2014. Empirical evaluation of gated recurrent neural networks on sequence modeling. In *Proceedings of NIPS 2014 Workshop on Deep Learning, December 2014*.

Fabien Cromieres. 2016. Kyoto-NMT: a neural machine translation implementation in chainer. In *Proceedings of COLING 2016, the 26th International Conference on Computational Linguistics: System Demonstrations*, pages 307–311, Osaka, Japan, December.

Isao Goto, Bin Lu, Ka Po Chow, Eiichiro Sumita, and Benjamin K. Tsou. 2011. Overview of the patent machine translation task at the NTCIR-9 workshop. In *Proceedings of NTCIR-9*, pages 559–578.

Isao Goto, Ka Po Chow, Bin Lu, Eiichiro Sumita, and Benjamin K. Tsou. 2013. Overview of the patent machine translation task at the NTCIR-10 workshop. In *Proceedings of NTCIR-10*, pages 260–286.

Sepp Hochreiter and Jürgen Schmidhuber. 1997. Long short-term memory. *Neural Computation*, 9(8):1735–1780.

Diederik P. Kingma and Jimmy Ba. 2014. Adam: A method for stochastic optimization. *CoRR*, abs/1412.6980.

Philipp Koehn, Franz J. Och, and Daniel Marcu. 2003. Statistical phrase-based translation. In *Proceedings of NAACL HLT 2013*.

Philipp Koehn, Hieu Hoang, Alexandra Birch, Chris Callison-Burch, Marcello Federico, Nicola Bertoldi, Brooke Cowan, Wade Shen, Christine Moran, Richard Zens, Chris Dyer, Ondrej Bojar, Alexandra Constantin, and Evan Herbst. 2007. Moses: Open source toolkit for statistical machine translation. In *Proceedings of the ACL Demo and Poster Sessions*, pages 177–180.

Philipp Koehn. 2004. Statistical significance tests for machine translation evaluation. In Dekang Lin and Dekai Wu, editors, *Proceedings of EMNLP 2004*, pages 388–395.

Jiwei Li and Dan Jurafsky. 2016. Mutual information and diverse decoding improve neural machine translation. *CoRR*, abs/1601.00372.

Haitao Mi, Baskaran Sankaran, Zhiguo Wang, and Abe Ittycheriah. 2016. Coverage embedding models for neural machine translation. In *Proceedings of the 2016 Conference on Empirical Methods in Natural Language Processing*, pages 955–960, Austin, Texas, November.

Kishore Papineni, Salim Roukos, Todd Ward, and Wei-Jing Zhu. 2002. Bleu: a Method for Automatic Evaluation of Machine Translation. In *Proceedings of ACL 2002*, pages 311–318.

Ilya Sutskever, Oriol Vinyals, and Quoc V Le. 2014. Sequence to sequence learning with neural networks. In *Advances in Neural Information Processing Systems 27*, pages 3104–3112.

Seiya Tokui, Kenta Oono, Shohei Hido, and Justin Clayton. 2015. Chainer: a next-generation open source framework for deep learning. In *Proceedings of Workshop on Machine Learning Systems (LearningSys) in The Twenty-ninth Annual Conference on Neural Information Processing Systems (NIPS)*.

Zhaopeng Tu, Yang Liu, Lifeng Shang, Xiaohua Liu, and Hang Li. 2016a. Neural machine translation with reconstruction. *CoRR*, abs/1611.01874.

Zhaopeng Tu, Zhengdong Lu, Yang Liu, Xiaohua Liu, and Hang Li. 2016b. Modeling coverage for neural machine translation. In *Proceedings of the 54th Annual Meeting of the Association for Computational Linguistics (Volume 1: Long Papers)*, pages 76–85, Berlin, Germany, August.

Yonghui Wu, Mike Schuster, Zhifeng Chen, Quoc V. Le, Mohammad Norouzi, Wolfgang Macherey, Maxim Krikun, Yuan Cao, Qin Gao, Klaus Macherey, Jeff Klingner, Apurva Shah, Melvin Johnson, Xiaobing Liu, Lukasz Kaiser, Stephan

Gouws, Yoshikiyo Kato, Taku Kudo, Hideto Kazawa, Keith Stevens, George Kurian, Nishant Patil, Wei Wang, Cliff Young, Jason Smith, Jason Riesa, Alex Rudnick, Oriol Vinyals, Greg Corrado, Macduff Hughes, and Jeffrey Dean. 2016. Google's neural machine translation system: Bridging the gap between human and machine translation. *CoRR*, abs/1609.08144.

# Beam Search Strategies for Neural Machine Translation

**Markus Freitag** and **Yaser Al-Onaizan**
IBM T.J. Watson Research Center
1101 Kitchawan Rd, Yorktown Heights, NY 10598
{freitagm,onaizan}@us.ibm.com

## Abstract

The basic concept in Neural Machine Translation (NMT) is to train a large Neural Network that maximizes the translation performance on a given parallel corpus. NMT is then using a simple left-to-right beam-search decoder to generate new translations that approximately maximize the trained conditional probability. The current beam search strategy generates the target sentence word by word from left-to-right while keeping a fixed amount of active candidates at each time step. First, this simple search is less adaptive as it also expands candidates whose scores are much worse than the current best. Secondly, it does not expand hypotheses if they are not within the best scoring candidates, even if their scores are close to the best one. The latter one can be avoided by increasing the beam size until no performance improvement can be observed. While you can reach better performance, this has the drawback of a slower decoding speed. In this paper, we concentrate on speeding up the decoder by applying a more flexible beam search strategy whose candidate size may vary at each time step depending on the candidate scores. We speed up the original decoder by up to 43% for the two language pairs German→English and Chinese→English without losing any translation quality.

## 1 Introduction

Due to the fact that Neural Machine Translation (NMT) is reaching comparable or even better performance compared to the traditional statistical machine translation (SMT) models (Jean et al.,

2015; Luong et al., 2015), it has become very popular in the recent years (Kalchbrenner and Blunsom, 2013; Sutskever et al., 2014; Bahdanau et al., 2014). With the recent success of NMT, attention has shifted towards making it more practical. One of the challenges is the search strategy for extracting the best translation for a given source sentence. In NMT, new sentences are translated by a simple beam search decoder that finds a translation that approximately maximizes the conditional probability of a trained NMT model. The beam search strategy generates the translation word by word from left-to-right while keeping a fixed number (beam) of active candidates at each time step. By increasing the beam size, the translation performance can increase at the expense of significantly reducing the decoder speed. Typically, there is a saturation point at which the translation quality does not improve any more by further increasing the beam. The motivation of this work is two folded. First, we prune the search graph, thus, speed up the decoding process without losing any translation quality. Secondly, we observed that the best scoring candidates often share the same history and often come from the same partial hypothesis. We limit the amount of candidates coming from the same partial hypothesis to introduce more diversity without reducing the decoding speed by just using a higher beam.

## 2 Related Work

The original beam search for sequence to sequence models has been introduced and described by (Graves, 2012; Boulanger-Lewandowski et al., 2013) and by (Sutskever et al., 2014) for neural machine translation. (Hu et al., 2015; Mi et al., 2016) improved the beam search with a constraint softmax function which only considered a limited word set of translation candidates to reduce



*Proceedings of the First Workshop on Neural Machine Translation*, pages 56–60,
Vancouver, Canada, August 4, 2017. ©2017 Association for Computational Linguistics

the computation complexity. This has the advantage that they normalize only a small set of candidates and thus improve the decoding speed. (Wu et al., 2016) only consider tokens that have local scores that are not more than beamsize below the best token during their search. Further, the authors prune all partial hypotheses whose score are beamsize lower than the best final hypothesis (if one has already been generated). In this work, we investigate different absolute and relative pruning schemes which have successfully been applied in statistical machine translation for e.g. phrase table pruning (Zens et al., 2012).

## 3 Original Beam Search

The original beam-search strategy finds a translation that approximately maximizes the conditional probability given by a specific model. It builds the translation from left-to-right and keeps a fixed number (beam) of translation candidates with the highest log-probability at each time step. For each end-of-sequence symbol that is selected among the highest scoring candidates the beam is reduced by one and the translation is stored into a final candidate list. When the beam is zero, it stops the search and picks the translation with the highest log-probability (normalized by the number of target words) out of the final candidate list.

## 4 Search Strategies

In this section, we describe the different strategies we experimented with. In all our extensions, we first reduce the candidate list to the current beam size and apply on top of this one or several of the following pruning schemes.

**Relative Threshold Pruning.** The relative threshold pruning method discards those candidates that are far worse than the best active candidate. Given a pruning threshold $rp$ and an active candidate list $C$, a candidate $cand \in C$ is discarded if:

$$score(cand) \leq rp * \max_{c \in C}\{score(c)\} \quad (1)$$

**Absolute Threshold Pruning.** Instead of taking the relative difference of the scores into account, we just discard those candidates that are worse by a specific threshold than the best active candidate. Given a pruning threshold $ap$ and an active candidate list $C$, a candidate $cand \in C$ is discarded if:

$$score(cand) \leq \max_{c \in C}\{score(c)\} - ap \quad (2)$$

**Relative Local Threshold Pruning.** In this pruning approach, we only consider the score $score_w$ of the last generated word and not the total score which also include the scores of the previously generated words. Given a pruning threshold $rpl$ and an active candidate list $C$, a candidate $cand \in C$ is discarded if:

$$score_w(cand) \leq rpl * \max_{c \in C}\{score_w(c)\} \quad (3)$$

**Maximum Candidates per Node** We observed that at each time step during the decoding process, most of the partial hypotheses share the same predecessor words. To introduce more diversity, we allow only a fixed number of candidates with the same history at each time step. Given a maximum candidate threshold $mc$ and an active candidate list $C$, a candidate $cand \in C$ is discarded if already $mc$ better scoring partial hyps with the same history are in the candidate list.

## 5 Experiments

For the German→English translation task, we train an NMT system based on the WMT 2016 training data (Bojar et al., 2016) (3.9M parallel sentences). For the Chinese→English experiments, we use an NMT system trained on 11 million sentences from the BOLT project.

In all our experiments, we use our in-house attention-based NMT implementation which is similar to (Bahdanau et al., 2014). For German→English, we use sub-word units extracted by byte pair encoding (Sennrich et al., 2015) instead of words which shrinks the vocabulary to 40k sub-word symbols for both source and target. For Chinese→English, we limit our vocabularies to be the top 300K most frequent words for both source and target language. Words not in these vocabularies are converted into an unknown token. During translation, we use the alignments (from the attention mechanism) to replace the unknown tokens either with potential targets (obtained from an IBM Model-1 trained on the parallel data) or with the source word itself (if no target was found) (Mi et al., 2016). We use an embedding dimension of 620 and fix the RNN GRU layers to be of 1000 cells each. For the training procedure, we use SGD (Bishop, 1995) to update model

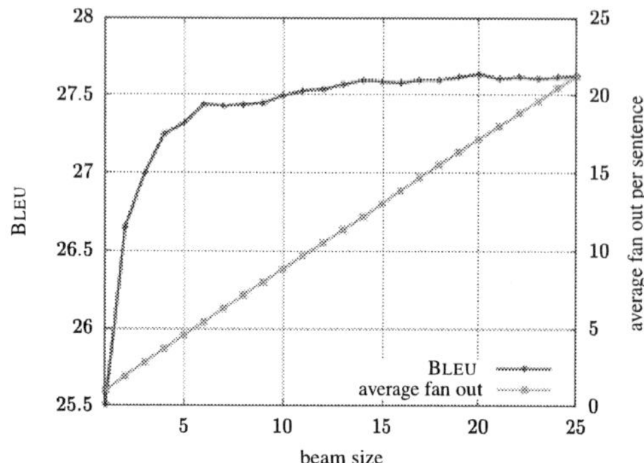

Figure 1: German→English: Original beam-search strategy with different beam sizes on new-stest2014.

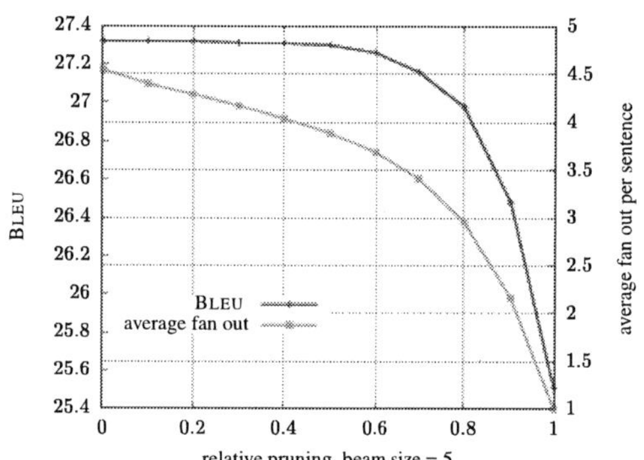

Figure 2: German→English: Different values of relative pruning measured on newstest2014.

parameters with a mini-batch size of 64. The training data is shuffled after each epoch.

We measure the decoding speed by two numbers. First, we compare the actual speed relative to the same setup without any pruning. Secondly, we measure the average fan out per time step. For each time step, the fan out is defined as the number of candidates we expand. Fan out has an upper bound of the size of the beam, but can be decreased either due to early stopping (we reduce the beam every time we predict a end-of-sentence symbol) or by the proposed pruning schemes. For each pruning technique, we run the experiments with different pruning thresholds and chose the largest threshold that did not degrade the translation performance based on a selection set.

In Figure 1, you can see the German→English translation performance and the average fan out per sentence for different beam sizes. Based on this experiment, we decided to run our pruning experiments for beam size 5 and 14. The

German→English results can be found in Table 1. By using the combination of all pruning techniques, we can speed up the decoding process by 13% for beam size 5 and by 43% for beam size 14 without any drop in performance. The relative pruning technique is the best working one for beam size 5 whereas the absolute pruning technique works best for a beam size 14. In Figure 2 the decoding speed with different relative pruning threshold for beam size 5 are illustrated. Setting the threshold higher than 0.6 hurts the translation performance. A nice side effect is that it has become possible to decode without any fix beam size when we apply pruning. Nevertheless, the decoding speed drops while the translation performance did not change. Further, we looked at the number of search errors introduced by our pruning schemes (number of times we prune the best scoring hypothesis). 5% of the sentences change due to search errors for beam size 5 and 9% of the sentences change for beam size 14 when using all four pruning techniques together.

The Chinese→English translation results can be found in Table 2. We can speed up the decoding process by 10% for beam size 5 and by 24% for beam size 14 without loss in translation quality. In addition, we measured the number of search errors introduced by pruning the search. Only 4% of the sentences change for beam size 5, whereas 22% of the sentences change for beam size 14.

## 6 Conclusion

The original beam search decoder used in Neural Machine Translation is very simple. It generated translations from left-to-right while looking at a fix number (beam) of candidates from the last time step only. By setting the beam size large enough, we ensure that the best translation performance can be reached with the drawback that many candidates whose scores are far away from the best are also explored. In this paper, we introduced several pruning techniques which prune candidates whose scores are far away from the best one. By applying a combination of absolute and relative pruning schemes, we speed up the decoder by up to 43% without losing any translation quality. Putting more diversity into the decoder did not improve the translation quality.

| pruning | beam size | speed up | avg fan out per sent | tot fan out per sent | newstest2014 | | newstest2015 | |
|---|---|---|---|---|---|---|---|---|
| | | | | | BLEU | TER | BLEU | TER |
| no pruning | 1 | - | 1.00 | 25 | 25.5 | 56.8 | 26.1 | 55.4 |
| no pruning | 5 | - | 4.54 | 122 | 27.3 | 54.6 | 27.4 | 53.7 |
| rp=0.6 | 5 | 6% | 3.71 | 109 | 27.3 | 54.7 | 27.3 | 53.8 |
| ap=2.5 | 5 | 5% | 4.11 | 116 | 27.3 | 54.6 | 27.4 | 53.7 |
| rpl=0.02 | 5 | 5% | 4.25 | 118 | 27.3 | 54.7 | 27.4 | 53.8 |
| mc=3 | 5 | 0% | 4.54 | 126 | 27.4 | 54.6 | 27.5 | 53.8 |
| rp=0.6,ap=2.5,rpl=0.02,mc=3 | 5 | 13% | 3.64 | 101 | 27.3 | 54.6 | 27.3 | 53.8 |
| no pruning | 14 | - | 12.19 | 363 | 27.6 | 54.3 | 27.6 | 53.5 |
| rp=0.3 | 14 | 10% | 10.38 | 315 | 27.6 | 54.3 | 27.6 | 53.4 |
| ap=2.5 | 14 | 29% | 9.49 | 279 | 27.6 | 54.3 | 27.6 | 53.5 |
| rpl=0.3 | 14 | 24% | 10.27 | 306 | 27.6 | 54.4 | 27.7 | 53.4 |
| mc=3 | 14 | 1% | 12.21 | 347 | 27.6 | 54.4 | 27.7 | 53.4 |
| rp=0.3,ap=2.5,rpl=0.3,mc=3 | 14 | 43% | 8.44 | 260 | 27.6 | 54.5 | 27.6 | 53.4 |
| rp=0.3,ap=2.5,rpl=0.3,mc=3 | - | - | 28.46 | 979 | 27.6 | 54.4 | 27.6 | 53.3 |

Table 1: Results German→English: relative pruning(rp), absolute pruning(ap), relative local pruning(rpl) and maximum candidates per node(mc). Average fan out is the average number of candidates we keep at each time step during decoding.

| pruning | beam size | speed up | avg fan out per sent | tot fan out per sent | MT08 nw | | MT08 wb | |
|---|---|---|---|---|---|---|---|---|
| | | | | | BLEU | TER | BLEU | TER |
| no pruning | 1 | - | 1.00 | 29 | 27.3 | 61.7 | 26.0 | 60.3 |
| no pruning | 5 | - | 4.36 | 137 | 34.4 | 57.3 | 30.6 | 58.2 |
| rp=0.2 | 5 | 1% | 4.32 | 134 | 34.4 | 57.3 | 30.6 | 58.2 |
| ap=5 | 5 | 4% | 4.26 | 132 | 34.3 | 57.3 | 30.6 | 58.2 |
| rpl=0.01 | 5 | 1% | 4.35 | 135 | 34.4 | 57.5 | 30.6 | 58.3 |
| mc=3 | 5 | 0% | 4.37 | 139 | 34.4 | 57.4 | 30.7 | 58.2 |
| rp=0.2,ap=5,rpl=0.01,mc=3 | 5 | 10% | 3.92 | 121 | 34.3 | 57.3 | 30.6 | 58.2 |
| no pruning | 14 | - | 11.96 | 376 | 35.3 | 57.1 | 31.2 | 57.8 |
| rp=0.2 | 14 | 3% | 11.62 | 362 | 35.2 | 57.2 | 31.2 | 57.8 |
| ap=2.5 | 14 | 14% | 10.15 | 321 | 35.2 | 56.9 | 31.1 | 57.9 |
| rpl=0.3 | 14 | 10% | 10.93 | 334 | 35.3 | 57.2 | 31.1 | 57.9 |
| mc=3 | 14 | 0% | 11.98 | 378 | 35.3 | 56.9 | 31.1 | 57.8 |
| rp=0.2,ap=2.5,rpl=0.3,mc=3 | 14 | 24% | 8.62 | 306 | 35.3 | 56.9 | 31.1 | 57.8 |
| rp=0.2,ap=2.5,rpl=0.3,mc=3 | - | - | 38.76 | 1411 | 35.2 | 57.3 | 31.1 | 57.9 |

Table 2: Results Chinese→English: relative pruning(rp), absolute pruning(ap), relative local pruning(rpl) and maximum candidates per node(mc).

# References


D. Bahdanau, K. Cho, and Y. Bengio. 2014. Neural machine translation by jointly learning to align and translate. *ArXiv e-prints* .

Christopher M Bishop. 1995. *Neural networks for pattern recognition*. Oxford university press.

Ondrej Bojar, Rajen Chatterjee, Christian Federmann, Yvette Graham, Barry Haddow, Matthias Huck, Antonio Jimeno Yepes, Philipp Koehn, Varvara Logacheva, Christof Monz, et al. 2016. Findings of the 2016 conference on machine translation (wmt16). *Proceedings of WMT* .

Nicolas Boulanger-Lewandowski, Yoshua Bengio, and Pascal Vincent. 2013. Audio chord recognition with recurrent neural networks. In *ISMIR*. Citeseer, pages 335–340.

Alex Graves. 2012. Sequence transduction with recurrent neural networks. *arXiv preprint arXiv:1211.3711* .

Xiaoguang Hu, Wei Li, Xiang Lan, Hua Wu, and

Haifeng Wang. 2015. Improved beam search with constrained softmax for nmt. *Proceedings of MT Summit XV* page 297.

Sébastien Jean, Kyunghyun Cho, Roland Memisevic, and Yoshua Bengio. 2015. On using very large target vocabulary for neural machine translation. In *Proceedings of ACL*. Beijing, China, pages 1–10.

Nal Kalchbrenner and Phil Blunsom. 2013. Recurrent continuous translation models. In *Proceedings of the 2013 Conference on Empirical Methods in Natural Language Processing*. Association for Computational Linguistics, Seattle.

Thang Luong, Ilya Sutskever, Quoc Le, Oriol Vinyals, and Wojciech Zaremba. 2015. Addressing the rare word problem in neural machine translation. In *Proceedings of ACL*. Beijing, China, pages 11–19.

Haitao Mi, Zhiguo Wang, and Abe Ittycheriah. 2016. Vocabulary manipulation for neural machine translation. *arXiv preprint arXiv:1605.03209* .

Rico Sennrich, Barry Haddow, and Alexandra Birch. 2015. Neural machine translation of rare words with subword units. *arXiv preprint arXiv:1508.07909* .

Ilya Sutskever, Oriol Vinyals, and Quoc V. Le. 2014. Sequence to sequence learning with neural networks. In *Advances in Neural Information Processing Systems 27: Annual Conference on Neural Information Processing Systems 2014, December 8-13 2014, Montreal, Quebec, Canada*. pages 3104–3112. http://papers.nips.cc/paper/5346-sequence-to-sequence-learning-with-neural-networks.

Yonghui Wu, Mike Schuster, Zhifeng Chen, Quoc V Le, Mohammad Norouzi, Wolfgang Macherey, Maxim Krikun, Yuan Cao, Qin Gao, Klaus Macherey, et al. 2016. Google's neural machine translation system: Bridging the gap between human and machine translation. *arXiv preprint arXiv:1609.08144* .

Richard Zens, Daisy Stanton, and Peng Xu. 2012. A systematic comparison of phrase table pruning techniques. In *Proceedings of the 2012 Joint Conference on Empirical Methods in Natural Language Processing and Computational Natural Language Learning*. Association for Computational Linguistics, pages 972–983.

# An Empirical Study of Mini-Batch Creation Strategies for Neural Machine Translation


**Makoto Morishita**[1][*]**, Yusuke Oda**[2]**, Graham Neubig**[3,2]**,**
**Koichiro Yoshino**[2,4]**, Katsuhito Sudoh**[2]**, Satoshi Nakamura**[2]

[1]NTT Communication Science Laboratories, NTT Corporation
[2]Nara Institute of Science and Technology
[3]Carnegie Mellon University
[4]PRESTO, Japan Science and Technology Agency

`morishita.makoto@lab.ntt.co.jp, gneubig@cs.cmu.edu`
`{oda.yusuke.on9, koichiro, sudoh, s-nakamura}@is.naist.jp`



## Abstract

Training of neural machine translation (NMT) models usually uses mini-batches for efficiency purposes. During the mini-batched training process, it is necessary to pad shorter sentences in a mini-batch to be equal in length to the longest sentence therein for efficient computation. Previous work has noted that sorting the corpus based on the sentence length before making mini-batches reduces the amount of padding and increases the processing speed. However, despite the fact that mini-batch creation is an essential step in NMT training, widely used NMT toolkits implement disparate strategies for doing so, which have not been empirically validated or compared. This work investigates mini-batch creation strategies with experiments over two different datasets. Our results suggest that the choice of a mini-batch creation strategy has a large effect on NMT training and some length-based sorting strategies do not always work well compared with simple shuffling.


## 1 Introduction

Mini-batch training is a standard practice in large-scale machine learning. In recent implementations of neural networks, the efficiency of loss and gradient calculation is greatly improved by mini-batching due to the fact that combining training examples into batches allows for fewer but larger operations that can take advantage of the parallelism allowed by modern computation architectures, particularly GPUs.

In some cases, such as the case of processing images, mini-batching is straightforward, as the inputs in all training examples take the same form. However, in order to perform mini-batching in the training of neural machine translation (NMT) or other sequence-to-sequence models, we need to *pad* shorter sentences to be the same length as the longest sentences to account for sentences of variable length in each mini-batch.

To help prevent wasted calculation due to this padding, it is common to sort the corpus according to the sentence length before creating mini-batches (Sutskever et al., 2014; Bahdanau et al., 2015), because putting sentences that have similar lengths in the same mini-batch will reduce the amount of padding and increase the per-word computation speed. However, we can also easily imagine that this grouping of sentences together may affect the convergence speed and stability, and the performance of the learned models. Despite this fact, no previous work has explicitly examined how mini-batch creation affects the learning of NMT models. Various NMT toolkits include implementations of different strategies, but they have neither been empirically validated nor compared.

In this work, we attempt to fill this gap by surveying the various mini-batch creation strategies that are in use: sorting by length of the source sentence, target sentence, or both, as well as making mini-batches according to the number of sentences and the number of words. We empirically compare their efficacy on two translation tasks and find that some strategies in wide use are not necessarily optimal for reliably training models.

## 2 Mini-batches for NMT

First, to clearly demonstrate the problem of mini-batching in NMT models, Figure 1 shows an ex-

---

[*] This work is done while the author was at Nara Institute of Science and Technology.




*Proceedings of the First Workshop on Neural Machine Translation*, pages 61–68,
Vancouver, Canada, August 4, 2017. ©2017 Association for Computational Linguistics

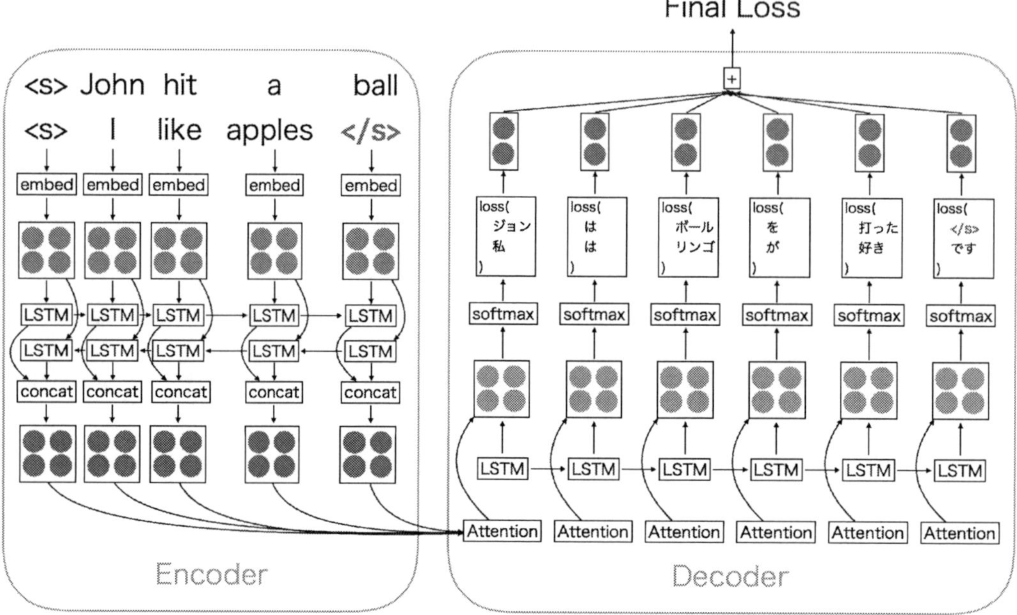



Figure 1: An example of mini-batching in an encoder-decoder translation model.

ample of mini-batching two sentences of different lengths in an encoder-decoder model.

The first thing that we can notice from the figure is that multiple operations at a particular time step $t$ can be combined into a single operation. For example, both "John" and "I" are embedded in a single step into a matrix that is passed into the encoder LSTM in a single step. On the target side as well, we calcualate the loss for the target words at time step $t$ for every sentence in the mini-batch simultaneously.

However, there are problems when sentences are of different length, as only some sentences will have any content at a particular time step. To resolve this problem, we pad short sentences with end-of-sentence tokens to adjust their length to the length of the longest sentence. In the Figure 1, purple colored "$\langle$/s$\rangle$" indicates the padded end-of-sentence token.

Padding with these tokens makes it possible to handle variably-lengthed sentences as if they were of the same length. On the other hand, the computational cost for a mini-batch increases in proportion to the longest sentence therein, and excess padding can result in a significant amount of wasted computation. One way to fix this problem is by creating mini-batches that include sentences of similar length (Sutskever et al., 2014)

---

**Algorithm 1** Create mini-batches

---

1: $C \leftarrow$ Training corpus
2: $C \leftarrow$ sort($C$) or shuffle($C$)  ▷ sort or shuffle the whole corpus
3: $B \leftarrow \{\}$  ▷ mini-batches
4: $i \leftarrow 0,\ j \leftarrow 0$
5: **while** $i < C$.size() **do**
6:     $B[j] \leftarrow B[j] + C[i]$
7:     **if** $B[j]$.size() $\geq$ max mini-batch size **then**
8:         $B[j] \leftarrow$ padding($B[j]$)  ▷ Padding tokens to the longest sentence in the mini-batch
9:         $j \leftarrow j + 1$
10:     **end if**
11:     $i \leftarrow i + 1$
12: **end while**
13: $B \leftarrow$ shuffle($B$)  ▷ shuffle the order of the mini-batches

---

to reduce the amount of padding required. Many NMT toolkits implement length-based sorting of the training corpus for this purpose. In the following section, we discuss several different mini-batch creation strategies used in existing neural MT toolkits.

## 3 Mini-batch Creation Strategies

Specifically, we examine three aspects of mini-batch creation: mini-batch size, word vs. sentence mini-batches, and sorting strategies. Algorithm 1 shows the pseudo code of creating mini-batches.

### 3.1 Mini-batch Size

The first aspect we consider is *mini-batch size* for which, of the three aspects we examine here, the effect is relatively well known.

When we use larger mini-batches, more sentences participate in the gradient calculation making the gradients more stable. They also increase efficiency with parallel computation. However, they decrease the number of parameter updates performed in a certain amount of time, which can slow convergence at the beginning of training. Large mini-batches can also pose problems in practice due to the fact that they increase memory requirements.

### 3.2 Sentence vs. Word Mini-batching

The second aspect that we examine, which has not been examined in detail previously, is whether to create mini-batches based on the *number of sentences* or *number of target words*.

Most NMT toolkits create mini-batches with a constant number of sentences. In this case, the number of words included in each mini-batch differs greatly due to the variance in sentence lengths. If we use the neural network library that constructs graphs in a dynamic fashion (e.g. DyNet (Neubig et al., 2017), Chainer (Tokui et al., 2015), or PyTorch[1]), this will lead to a large variance in memory consumption from mini-batch to mini-batch. In addition, because the loss function for the mini-batch is equal to the sum of the losses incurred for each word, the scale of the losses will vary greatly from mini-batch to mini-batch, which could be potentially detrimental to training.

Another choice is to create mini-batches by keeping the number of target words in each mini-batch approximately stable, but varying the number of sentences. We hypothesize that this may lead to more stable convergence, and test this hypothesis in the experiments.

### 3.3 Corpus Sorting Methods

The final aspect that we examine, which has similarly is not yet well understood, is the effect of

---

[1] http://pytorch.org

*the method that we use to sort the corpus before grouping consecutive sentences into mini-batches.*

A standard practice in online learning shuffles training samples to ensure that bias in the presentation order does not adversely affect the final result. However, as we mentioned in Section 2, NMT studies (Sutskever et al., 2014; Bahdanau et al., 2015) prefer uniform length samples in the mini-batch by sorting the training corpus, to reduce the amount of padding and increase per-word calculation speed. In particular, in the encoder-decoder NMT framework (Sutskever et al., 2014), the computational cost in the softmax layer of the decoder is much heavier than the encoder. Some NMT toolkits sort the training corpus based on the target sentence length to avoid unnecessary softmax computations on padded tokens in the target side. Another problem arises in the attentional NMT model (Bahdanau et al., 2015; Luong et al., 2015); attentions may give incorrect positive weights to the padded tokens in the source side. The problems above also motivate the mini-batch creation with uniform length sentences with fewer padded tokens.

Inspired by sorting methods in use in current open source implementations, we compare the following sorting methods:

**SHUFFLE:** Shuffle the corpus randomly before creating mini-batches, with no sorting.
**SRC:** Sort based on the source sentence length.
**TRG:** Sort based on the target sentence length.
**SRC_TRG:** Sort using the source sentence length, break ties by sorting by target sentence length.
**TRG_SRC:** Converse of SRC_TRG.

Of established open-source toolkits, OpenNMT (Klein et al., 2017) uses the SRC sorting method, Nematus[2] and KNMT (Cromieres, 2016) use the TRG sorting method, and lamtram[3] uses the TRG_SRC sorting method.

## 4 Experiments

We conducted NMT experiments with the strategies presented above to examine their effects on NMT training.

### 4.1 Experimental Settings

We carried out experiments with two language pairs, English-Japanese using the ASPEC-JE cor-

---

[2] https://github.com/rsennrich/nematus
[3] https://github.com/neubig/lamtram

|       | ASPEC-JE | WMT 2016 |
|-------|----------|----------|
| train | 2,000,000 | 4,562,102 |
| dev   | 1,790    | 2,169    |
| test  | 1,812    | 2,999    |

Table 1: Number of sentences in the corpus

pus (Nakazawa et al., 2016) and English-German using the WMT 2016 news task with newstest2016 as the test-set (Bojar et al., 2016). Table 1 shows the number of sentences contained in the corpora.

The English and German texts were tokenized with `tokenizer.perl`[4], and the Japanese texts were tokenized with KyTea (Neubig et al., 2011).

As a testbed for our experiments, we used the standard global attention model of Luong et al. (2015) with attention feeding and a bidirectional encoder with one LSTM layer of 512 nodes. We used the DyNet-based (Neubig et al., 2017) NMTKit[5], with a vocabulary size of 65536 words and dropout of 30% for all vertical connections. We used the same random numbers as initial parameters for each experiment to reduce variance due to initialization. We used Adam (Kingma and Ba, 2015) ($\alpha = 0.001$) or SGD ($\eta = 0.1$) as the learning algorithm. After every 50,000 training sentences, we processed the test set to record negative log likelihoods. In the testing, we set the mini-batch size to 1, in order to calculate negative log likelihood correctly. We calculated the case-insensitive BLEU score (Papineni et al., 2002) with `multi-bleu.perl`[6] script.

Table 2 shows the mini-batch creation settings compared in this paper, and we tried all sorting methods discussed in Section 3.3 for each setting. In method (e), we set the average number of target words in 64 sentences: 2055 words for ASPEC-JE, 1742 words for WMT. For all experiments, we shuffled the processing order of the mini-batches.

## 4.2 Experimental Results and Analysis

Figure 2, 3, 4 and 5 show the transition of negative log likelihoods and the BLEU scores according to the number of processed sentences in ASPEC-JE

|     | mini-batch units | learning algorithm |
|-----|------------------|--------------------|
| (a) | 64 sentences     | Adam               |
| (b) | 32 sentences     | Adam               |
| (c) | 16 sentences     | Adam               |
| (d) | 8 sentences      | Adam               |
| (e) | 2055 or 1742 words | Adam             |
| (f) | 64 sentences     | SGD                |

Table 2: Compared settings

| sorting method | average time (hour) |
|----------------|---------------------|
| SHUFFLE        | 8.08                |
| SRC            | 6.45                |
| TRG            | 5.21                |
| SRC_TRG        | 4.35                |
| TRG_SRC        | 4.30                |

Table 3: Average time needed to train a whole ASPEC-JE corpus using method (a). We used a GTX 1080 GPU for this experiment.

and WMT2016 test sets. Table 3 shows the average time to process the whole ASPEC-JE corpus.

The learning curves show very similar tendencies in different language pairs. We discuss the results in detail on each strategy that we investigated.

### 4.2.1 Effect of Mini-batch Size

We carried out the experiments with the mini-batch size of 8 to 64 sentences.[7]

From the experimental results of the method (a), (b), (c) and (d), in the case of using Adam, the mini-batch size affects the training speed and it also has an impact on the final accuracy of the model. As we mentioned in Section 3.1, the gradients can be stabler by increasing the mini-batch size, and it seems to have a positive impact on the model from the view of accuracy. Thus, we can first note that mini-batch size is a very important hyper-parameter for NMT training that should not be ignored. In our case in particular, the largest mini-batch size that could be loaded into the memory was the best for the NMT training.

### 4.2.2 Effect of Mini-batch Unit

Looking at the experimental results of the methods (a) and (e), we can see that perplexities drop faster if we use SHUFFLE for method (a) and SRC for method (e), but we couldn't see any large differences in terms of the training speed and the final

---

[4] `https://github.com/moses-smt/mosesdecoder/blob/master/scripts/tokenizer/tokenizer.perl`

[5] `https://github.com/odashi/nmtkit` We used the commit number `566e9c2`.

[6] `https://github.com/moses-smt/mosesdecoder/blob/master/scripts/generic/multi-bleu.perl`

[7] We tried the experiments with larger mini-batch size, but we couldn't run it due to the GPU memory limitation.

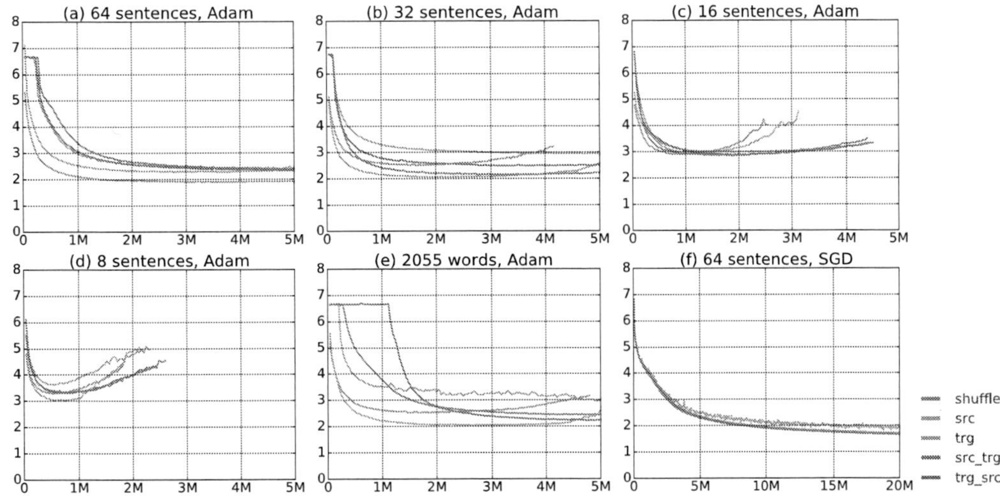

Figure 2: Training curves on the ASPEC-JE test set. The y- and x-axes shows the negative log likelihoods and number of processed sentences. The scale of the x-axis in the method (f) is different from others.

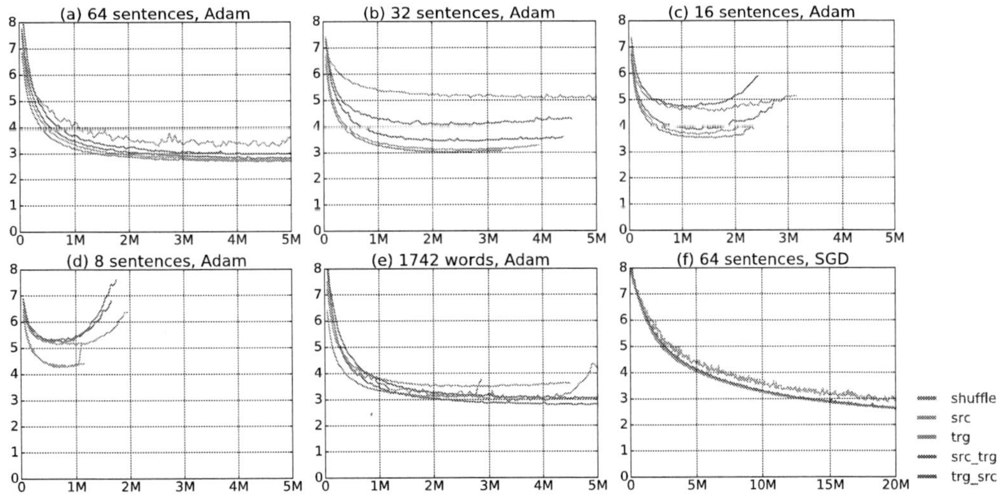

Figure 3: Training curves on the WMT2016 test set. Axes are the same as Figure 2.

accuracy of the model. We hypothesize that the large variance of the loss affects the final model accuracy, especially when using the learning algorithm that uses momentum such as Adam. However, these results indicate that these differences do not significantly affect the training results. We leave a comparison of memory consumption for future research.

### 4.2.3 Effect of Corpus Sorting Method using Adam

From all experimental results of the method (a), (b), (c), (d) and (e), in the case of using SHUF-FLE or SRC, perplexities drop faster and tend to converge to lower perplexities than the other methods for all mini-batch sizes. We believe the main reason for this is due to the similarity of the sentences contained in each mini-batch. If the sentence length is similar, the features of the sentence may also be similar. We carefully examined the corpus and found that at least this is true for the corpus we used (e.g. shorter sentences tend to contain the similar words). In this case, if we sort sentences by their length, sentences that have similar features will be gathered into the same mini-batch, making training less stable than if all sentences

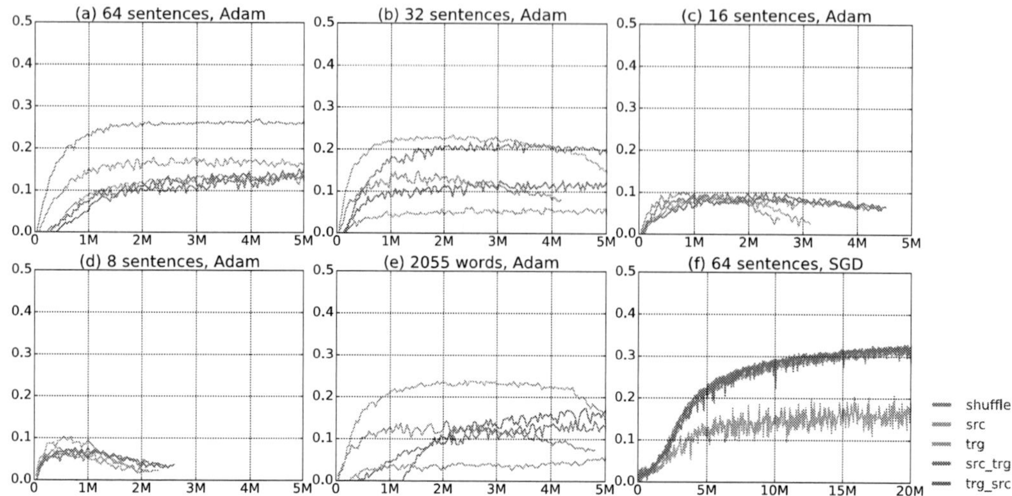

Figure 4: BLEU scores on the ASPEC-JE test set. The y- and x-axes shows the BLEU scores and number of processed sentences. The scale of the x-axis in the method (f) is different from others.

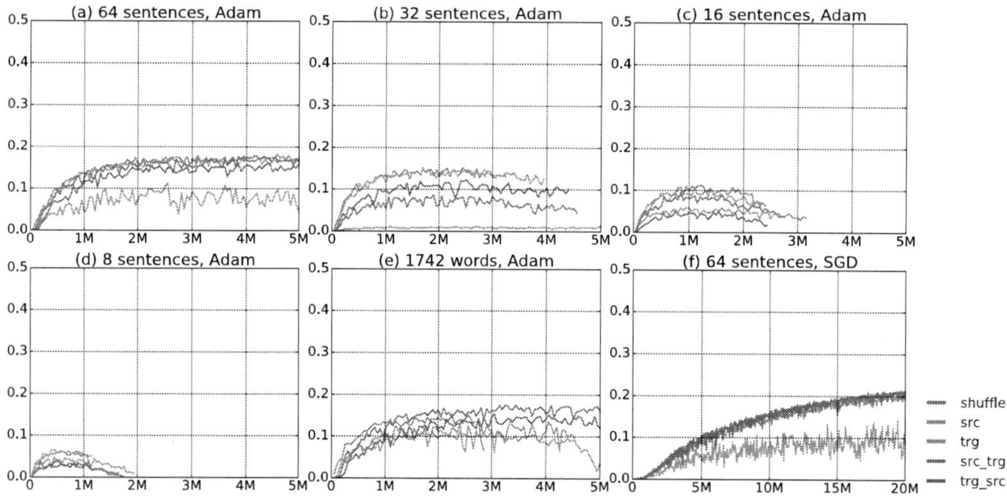

Figure 5: BLEU scores on the WMT2016 test set. Axes are the same as Figure 4.

in the mini-batch had different features. This is evidenced by the more jagged lines of the TRG method.

As a conclusion, the TRG and TRG_SRC sorting methods, which are used by many NMT toolkits, have a higher overall throughput when just measuring the number of words processed, but for convergence speed and final model accuracy, it seems to be better to use SHUFFLE or SRC.

Some toolkits shuffle the corpus first, then create mini-batches by sorting a few consecutive sentences. We think that this method may be effective by combining the advantage of SHUFFLE and other

sorting methods, but an empirical comparison is beyond the scope of this work.

### 4.2.4 Effect of Corpus Sorting Method using SGD

By comparing the experimental results of the methods (a) and (f), we found that in the case of using Adam, the learning curves greatly depend on the sorting method, but in the case of using SGD there was little effect. This is likely because SGD makes less bold updates of rare parameters, improving its overall stability. However, we find that only when using the TRG method, the nega-

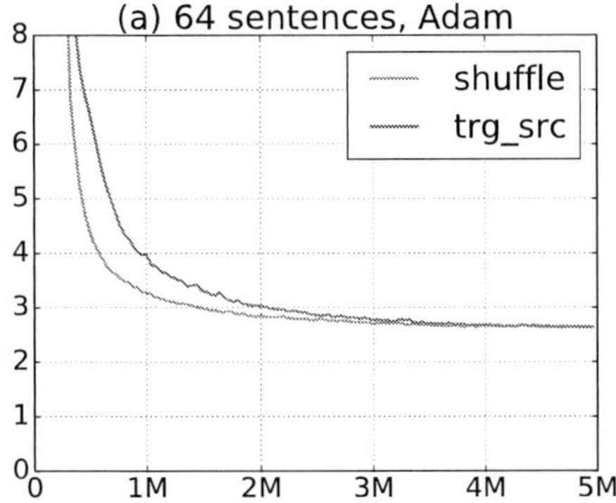


Figure 6: Training curves on the ASPEC test set using lamtram toolkit. Axes are the same as Figure 2.

tive log likelihoods and the BLEU scores are not stable. It can be conjectured that this is an effect of gathering the similar sentences in a mini-batch as we mentioned in Section 4.2.3. These results indicate that in the case of SGD it is acceptable to TRG_SRC, which is the fastest method to process the whole corpus (see Table 3), for SGD.

Recently, Wu et al. (2016) proposed a new learning paradigm, which uses Adam for the initial training, then switches to SGD after several iterations. If we use this learning algorithm, we may be able to train the model more effectively by using SHUFFLE or SRC sorting method for Adam, and TRG_SRC for SGD.

## 4.3 Experiments with a Different Toolkit

In the previous experiments, we conducted the experiments with only one NMT toolkit, so the results may be dependent on the particular implementation provided therein. To ensure that these results generalize to other toolkits with different default parameters, we conducted the experiments with another NMT toolkit.

### 4.3.1 Experimental Settings

In this section, we used lamtram[8] as a NMT toolkit. We carried out the Japanese-English translation experiments with ASPEC-JE corpus. We used Adam (Kingma and Ba, 2015) ($\alpha = 0.001$) as the learning algorithm and tried the two sorting algorithms: SHUFFLE which is the best sorting method on previous experiments and TRG_SRC which is the default sorting method used by the

lamtram toolkit. Normally, lamtram creates mini-batches based on the number of target words contained in each mini-batch, but we changed it to fix the mini-batch size to 64 sentences because we find that larger mini-batch size seems to be better in the previous experiments. Other experimental settings are the same as described in the Section 4.1.

### 4.3.2 Experimental Results

Figure 6 shows the transition of negative log likelihoods using lamtram. We can see the tendency of the training curves are similar to the Figure 2 (a), the combination with SHUFFLE drops negative log likelihood faster than the TRG_SRC one.

From this experiments, we could verify that our experimental results in the Section 4 do not rely on the toolkit and we think the observed behavior will generalize to other toolkits and implementations.

## 5 Related Work

Recently, Britz et al. (2017) have released a paper about exploring the hyper-parameters of NMT. This work is similar to our paper in the terms of finding the better hyper-parameters by doing a large number of experiments and deriving empirical conclusions. However, notably this paper fixed the mini-batch size to 128 sentences and did not treat mini-batch creation strategy as one of the hyper-parameters of the model. With our experimental results, we argue that the mini-batch creation strategies also have an impact on the NMT training, and thus having solid recommendations for how to adjust this hyper-parameter are also of merit.

## 6 Conclusion

In this paper, we analyzed how mini-batch creation strategies affect the training of NMT models for two language pairs. The experimental results suggest mini-batch creation strategy is an important hyper-parameter of the training process, and commonly-used sorting strategies are not always optimal. We sum up the results as follows:

- Mini-batch size can affect the final accuracy of the model in addition to the training speed and the larger mini-batch size seems to be better.

- Mini-batch units do not effect to the training process, so it is possible to use either the number of sentences or target words.

- We should use SHUFFLE or SRC sorting method for Adam, and it is sufficient to use TRG_SRC for SGD.

In the future, we plan to do experiments with larger mini-batch sizes and compare the used peak memory between making mini-batches by the number of sentences or target words. We are also interested in checking the effects of different mini-batch creation strategies with other language pairs, corpora and optimization functions.

## Acknowledgments

This work was done as a part of the joint research project with NTT and Nara Institute of Science and Technology. This research has been supported in part by JSPS KAKENHI Grant Number 16H05873. We thank the anonymous reviewers for their insightful comments.

## References

Dzmitry Bahdanau, Kyunghyun Cho, and Yoshua Bengio. 2015. Neural machine translation by jointly learning to align and translate. In *Proceedings of the 3rd International Conference on Learning Representations (ICLR)*.

Ondřej Bojar, Rajen Chatterjee, Christian Federmann, Yvette Graham, Barry Haddow, Matthias Huck, Antonio Jimeno Yepes, Philipp Koehn, Varvara Logacheva, Christof Monz, Matteo Negri, Aurelie Neveol, Mariana Neves, Martin Popel, Matt Post, Raphael Rubino, Carolina Scarton, Lucia Specia, Marco Turchi, Karin Verspoor, and Marcos Zampieri. 2016. Findings of the 2016 conference on machine translation. In *Proceedings of the 1st Conference on Machine Translation (WMT)*.

Denny Britz, Anna Goldie, Minh-Thang Luong, and Quoc V. Le. 2017. Massive exploration of neural machine translation architectures. *arXiv preprint arXiv:1703.03906* .

Fabièn Cromieres. 2016. Kyoto-NMT: a neural machine translation implementation in chainer. In *Proceedings of the 26th International Conference on Computational Linguistics (COLING)*.

Diederik Kingma and Jimmy Ba. 2015. Adam: A method for stochastic optimization. In *Proceedings of the 3rd International Conference on Learning Representations (ICLR)*.

Guillaume Klein, Yoon Kim, Yuntian Deng, Jean Senellart, and Alexander M. Rush. 2017. OpenNMT: Open-source toolkit for neural machine translation. *arXiv preprint arXiv:1701.02810* .

Minh-Thang Luong, Hieu Pham, and Christopher D. Manning. 2015. Effective approaches to attention-based neural machine translation. In *Proceedings of the Conference on Empirical Methods in Natural Language Processing (EMNLP)*.

Toshiaki Nakazawa, Manabu Yaguchi, Kiyotaka Uchimoto, Masao Utiyama, Eiichiro Sumita, Sadao Kurohashi, and Hitoshi Isahara. 2016. ASPEC: Asian scientific paper excerpt corpus. In *Proceedings of the 10th International Conference on Language Resources and Evaluation (LREC)*.

Graham Neubig, Chris Dyer, Yoav Goldberg, Austin Matthews, Waleed Ammar, Antonios Anastasopoulos, Miguel Ballesteros, David Chiang, Daniel Clothiaux, Trevor Cohn, Kevin Duh, Manaal Faruqui, Cynthia Gan, Dan Garrette, Yangfeng Ji, Lingpeng Kong, Adhiguna Kuncoro, Gaurav Kumar, Chaitanya Malaviya, Paul Michel, Yusuke Oda, Matthew Richardson, Naomi Saphra, Swabha Swayamdipta, and Pengcheng Yin. 2017. DyNet: The dynamic neural network toolkit. *arXiv preprint arXiv:1701.03980* .

Graham Neubig, Yosuke Nakata, and Shinsuke Mori. 2011. Pointwise prediction for robust, adaptable Japanese morphological analysis. In *Proceedings of the 49th Annual Meeting of the Association for Computational Linguistics (ACL)*.

Kishore Papineni, Salim Roukos, Todd Ward, and Wei-Jing Zhu. 2002. BLEU: a method for automatic evaluation of machine translation. In *Proceedings of the 40th Annual Meeting of the Association for Computational Linguistics (ACL)*.

Ilya Sutskever, Oriol Vinyals, and Quoc V. Le. 2014. Sequence to sequence learning with neural networks. In *Proceedings of the 28th Annual Conference on Neural Information Processing Systems (NIPS)*.

Seiya Tokui, Kenta Oono, Shohei Hido, and Justin Clayton. 2015. Chainer: a next-generation open source framework for deep learning. In *Proceedings of Workshop on Machine Learning Systems (LearningSys) in The Twenty-ninth Annual Conference on Neural Information Processing Systems (NIPS)*.

Yonghui Wu, Mike Schuster, Zhifeng Chen, Quoc V. Le, Mohammad Norouzi, Wolfgang Macherey, Maxim Krikun, Yuan Cao, Qin Gao, Klaus Macherey, Jeff Klingner, Apurva Shah, Melvin Johnson, Xiaobing Liu, Łukasz Kaiser, Stephan Gouws, Yoshikiyo Kato, Taku Kudo, Hideto Kazawa, Keith Stevens, George Kurian, Nishant Patil, Wei Wang, Cliff Young, Jason Smith, Jason Riesa, Alex Rudnick, Oriol Vinyals, Greg Corrado, Macduff Hughes, and Jeffrey Dean. 2016. Google's neural machine translation system: Bridging the gap between human and machine translation. *arXiv preprint arXiv:1609.08144* .

# Detecting Cross-Lingual Semantic Divergence
## for Neural Machine Translation


**Marine Carpuat** and **Yogarshi Vyas** and **Xing Niu**
Department of Computer Science
University of Maryland
College Park, MD
{marine,yogarshi,xingniu}@cs.umd.edu



## Abstract

Parallel corpora are often not as parallel as one might assume: non-literal translations and noisy translations abound, even in curated corpora routinely used for training and evaluation. We use a cross-lingual textual entailment system to distinguish sentence pairs that are parallel in meaning from those that are not, and show that filtering out divergent examples from training improves translation quality.


## 1 Introduction

Parallel sentence pairs provide examples of translation equivalence to train Machine Translation (MT) and cross-lingual Natural Language Processing. However, despite what the term "parallel" implies, the source and target language often do not convey the exact same meaning. This is a surprisingly common phenomenon, not only in noisy corpora automatically extracted from comparable collections, but also in parallel training and test corpora, as can be seen in Table 1.

This issue has mostly been ignored in machine translation, where parallel sentences are assumed to be translations of each other, and translations are assumed to have the same meaning. Prior work on characterizing parallel sentences for MT has focused on data selection and weighting for domain adaptation (Foster and Kuhn, 2007; Axelrod et al., 2011, among others), and on assessing the relevance of parallel sentences by comparison with a corpus of interest. In contrast, we focus on detecting an intrinsic property of parallel sentence pairs. Divergent sentence pairs have been viewed as noise both in comparable and non-parallel corpora (Fung and Cheung, 2004; Munteanu and Marcu, 2005; Abdul-Rauf and Schwenk, 2009; Smith et al., 2010; Riesa and Marcu, 2012) and

| Divergent segments in OpenSubtitles | |
|---|---|
| en | someone wanted to cook bratwurst. |
| fr | vous vouliez des saucisses grillées. |
| gl | you wanted some grilled sausages. |
| en | i don't know what i'm gonna do. |
| fr | j'en sais rien. |
| gl | i don't know. |
| en | - has the sake chilled? - no, it's fine. |
| fr | - c'est assez chaud? |
| gl | - it is hot enough? |
| en | you help me with zander and i helped you with joe. |
| fr | tu m'as aidée avec zander, je t'ai aidée avec joe. |
| gl | you helped me with zander, i helped you with joe. |

| Divergent segments in newstest2012 | |
|---|---|
| en | i know they did. |
| fr | je le sais. |
| gl | i know it. |
| en | the female employee suffered from shock. |
| fr | les victimes ont survécu leur peur. |
| gl | the victims have survived their fear. |

Table 1: Parallel segments are not always semantically equivalent, as can be seen in these examples (English sentence (en), French sentence (fr) and its gloss (gl)) drawn from a random sample of OpenSubtitles and of the newstest2012 test set (Bojar et al., 2016).

in parallel corpora (Okita et al., 2009; Jiang et al., 2010; Denkowski et al., 2012).In contrast, we hypothesize that the translation process inherently introduces divergences that affect meaning, and that semantically divergent examples should be expected in all parallel corpora.

We show that semantically divergent examples significantly impact the learning curves and translation quality of neural machine translation systems. We repurpose the task of cross-lingual textual entailment (Mehdad et al., 2010) to automatically identify and filter divergent parallel sentence pairs from the OpenSubtitles corpus (Lison and Tiedemann, 2016). This approach outperforms




*Proceedings of the First Workshop on Neural Machine Translation*, pages 69–79,
Vancouver, Canada, August 4, 2017. ©2017 Association for Computational Linguistics

other data selection criterion, and even a system trained on twice as much data for two test genres.

## 2 Non-Divergence as a Data Selection Criterion

### 2.1 Motivation

We conjecture that training sequence-to-sequence models with attention for neural machine translation (Bahdanau et al., 2015; Sennrich et al., 2017) is more sensitive to divergent parallel examples than traditional phrase-based systems. Phrase-based systems are remarkably robust to noise in parallel segments: Goutte et al. (2012) showed that when introducing noise by permuting the target side of parallel pairs, as many as 30% of training examples had to be noisy to hurt BLEU score significantly. However, such artificial noise does not capture naturally occurring divergences, which are likely to be more subtle. Syntax-based systems have been shown to be sensitive to divergences when they generate word-alignment errors: for instance, using syntax to eliminate word alignment links that violate syntactic correspondences yields better string-to-tree transducer rules, and better translation quality (Fossum et al., 2008).

In contrast, there is evidence that deep neural networks are sensitive to the nature and order of training examples in various related settings. On image classification benchmarks, Zhang et al. (2017) show that convolutional neural networks have the capacity to memorize versions of the training data corrupted in various ways, including random labelings of the original images, and random transformations of the input images. This suggests that neural models might attempt to memorize the idiosyncrasies of divergent parallel segments, which might hurt generalization at test time. In machine translation, domain adaptation results (Durrani et al., 2016) show that neural models benefit from early training on the United Nations corpus before fine-tuning on in-domain data, while the UN corpus is generally considered to be too distant from any domain that is not UN to be useful when training e.g., phrase-based systems. Online training also motivates curriculum learning approaches: ordering examples from easier short sentences to harder long sentences has also been found advantageous for neural language modeling (Bengio et al., 2009).

Most directly related to this work, Chen et al. (2016) suggest that neural MT systems are more sensitive to sentence pair permutations than phrase-based systems (Goutte et al., 2012). They also show that a bilingual convolutional neural network trained to discriminate in-domain from out-of-domain sentence pairs effectively selects training data that is not only in domain but also less noisy. These results provide further evidence that the degree of parallelism in training examples has an impact in neural MT. Yet it remains to be seen to what extent semantic divergences – rather than noise – affect translation quality in general – and not only in domain adaptation settings.

### 2.2 Approach

In this paper, we seek to measure the impact of semantic divergence on translation quality when used as a data selection criterion: if our hypothesis holds, then training on non-divergent examples should yield better translation quality than training on the same number of examples selected using other criteria. Unlike in domain adaptation, semantic divergence is an intrinsic property of a parallel sentence pair, and is therefore independent of domains or specific testing conditions. As we will see, we treat the detection of the divergent examples as a classification problem. Training examples can be ranked based on the confidence of the classifier that the segment contains two sentences that are not equivalent in meaning, and use the resulting ranking to filter out examples.

In addition, data selection can help address practical concerns. Training neural machine translation systems on large scale parallel corpora has a prohibitive computational cost. For instance, the winning neural systems at the WMT evaluation required two weeks of training (Sennrich et al., 2016a). Automatically identifying the most useful training examples has the potential to reduce training time significantly.

## 3 Detecting Semantic Divergences in Parallel Segments

We aim to automatically detect whether the source and target side of a parallel example are semantically equivalent. Since parallel corpora are not readily annotated with semantic equivalence, we repurpose related cross-lingual semantic annotations and models for this task.

## 3.1 Model

We frame the task of detecting whether parallel sentences $(e, f)$ are equivalent as a classification problem. We draw inspiration from related work on semantic textual similarity (Agirre et al., 2016), translation quality estimation (Hildebrand and Vogel, 2013), parallel sentence detection (Munteanu and Marcu, 2006) to design simple features that can be induced without supervision.

First, differences in sentence lengths are strong indicators of divergence in content between $e$ and $f$. Accordingly, we use four length features: $|e|$, $|f|$, $\frac{|e|}{|f|}$, and $\frac{|f|}{|e|}$.

Second, we assume that the configuration of word alignment links between parallel sentences $(e, f)$ is indicative of equivalence: if $e$ and $f$ have the same meaning, then they will be easier to align. Accordingly, we compute the following features for each of $e$ and $f$:

- Ratio of aligned words
- Ratio of unaligned words
- Ratio of unaligned content words (defined as words that do not appear in a stopword list)
- Number of unaligned contiguous sequences
- Length of longest contiguous unaligned sequence
- Average length of aligned sequences
- Average length of unaligned sequences

## 3.2 Semantic Supervision

We use annotations of Cross-Lingual Textual Entailment (Mehdad et al., 2010). This task is framed as a four-way classification task. Given sentences $e$ and $f$, the goal is to predict whether (1) $e$ entails $f$, (2) $f$ entails $e$, (3) $e$ and $f$ both entail each other, (4) there is no entailment relation between $e$ and $f$. Negri and Mehdad (2010) showed that English training and test sets can be created by crowdsourcing, that are then translated to obtain cross-lingual datasets. Training and test data were made available at SemEval 2012 and 2013 (Negri et al., 2012, 2013). We hypothesize that examples detected as class (4) are the most divergent examples that are the least useful for training machine translation systems. While the 4-way classification task is more complex than our end goal of detecting divergent examples, we found that the 4-way classifier detects divergent examples from class (4) better than binary classifiers trained on various partitions of the 4-way training data.

Other relevant semantic annotations of bilingual corpora include cross-lingual semantic textual similarity (Agirre et al., 2016) and machine translation quality estimation datasets (Specia et al., 2010). The latter is not a good fit as it annotates machine translation output. The former is a better match but only provides test examples.

## 4 Experimental Settings

### 4.1 Divergence Detection Model Settings

We use the cross-lingual textual entailment datasets released at SemEval (Negri et al., 2012, 2013). The 2012 dataset consists of 1000 sentences per language, with equal train and test splits, while the 2013 dataset consists of 1500 sentences per language, 500 of which have been marked as the test set. All datasets are balanced across the four entailment classes.

Word alignments for features are trained on the Europarl corpus and the News Commentary corpus [1], with a total of 2.2M sentence pairs. We use symmetrized IBM 4 alignments obtained via MGIZA++, and obtain alignments for the CLTE data as well as the OpenSubtitles data by transductive training.

The classifier is the linear SVM implementation from Scikit-Learn [2] with $C = 1.0$ and a one-vs-rest multi-class scheme for 4-way classification.

### 4.2 Machine Translation Task and System

We evaluate on the English-French Microsoft Spoken Language Translation task (Federmann and Lewis, 2016), which provides a translation scenario motivated by real world applications. Following prior work (Farajian et al., 2016; Lewis et al., 2016), training data is drawn from the OpenSubtitles corpus (Lison and Tiedemann, 2016). The subtitle genre is also appropriate as it presents many potential divergences due to genre-specific constraints (Tiedemann, 2007). In addition, the robustness of the models is evaluated by testing on a second domain, leveraging publicly available TED talks test data (Cettolo et al., 2012). French and English sides of the corpus are uncased and tokenized using Moses preprocessing tools, and segmented using byte pair encoding (Sennrich et al., 2016b).

---

[1] `http://www.statmt.org/wmt15/training-parallel-nc-v10.tgz`
[2] `http://scikit-learn.org/stable/`

| Corpus | # Sentences | English | | French | |
|---|---|---|---|---|---|
| | | \|vocab\| | # tokens | \|vocab\| | # tokens |
| *Training Sets (Open Subtitles)* | | | | | |
| non-divergent | 17M | 63917 | 133.7M | 79818 | 133.6M |
| random | 17M | 64640 | 146.9M | 80222 | 139.1M |
| natural | 17M | 64495 | 147.3M | 77646 | 137.4M |
| length $< 10$ | 22M | 63643 | 133.0M | 79264 | 127.2M |
| all | 33.5M | 66935 | 288.5M | 82564 | 273.2M |
| *Test Sets* | | | | | |
| MSLT | 5292 | 3739 | 45197 | 4389 | 49562 |
| TED | 1305 | 3987 | 25466 | 4481 | 27513 |

Table 2: Data statistics for training and test sets. At train time, selecting non-divergent sentences yields (1) a smaller vocabulary compared to datasets of the same size (2) richer examples than selection based on length only, with a more diverse vocabulary.

The neural machine translation system is the encoder-decoder with attention implemented in Nematus (Sennrich et al., 2017), with suggested parameters. We use a vocabulary size of 90000, dimensions of word embeddings and hidden units are 500 and 1024 respectively. Models are trained using Adadelta (Zeiler, 2012), with a learning rate of 0.0001, a batch size of 80, and reshuffling at each epoch. Dropout is enabled. We use the first 5th of the MSLT test set as a validation set, and save models every 30000 updates.

### 4.3 Experimental Conditions

We empirically evaluate the impact of divergence on translation quality by considering the following experimental conditions, which correspond to different training sets for the same neural MT model and training configuration:

- NON-DIVERGENT filtering out the most divergent half of the training data
- RANDOM randomly downsampling the training corpus to half its size
- NATURAL use the natural order of the corpus files to select the first half of the corpus
- LENGTH select examples of length shorter than 10 words (the average sent length in the corpus)
- ALL default condition which uses the entire training corpus.

Training data statistics and their coverage of the test set are summarized in Table 2. Data selection naturally reduces the vocabulary size available compared to using all the training data, by at most 10%. Selecting non-divergent sentences yields a smaller vocabulary compared to using the same number of parallel sentence pairs selected based on natural order or random sampling. At the same time, non-divergent examples are richer than those selected based on length alone, with a more diverse vocabulary.

Test data statistics shows the complementarity of the two test conditions considered: the MSLT task consists of shorter sentences similarly to all training settings, while the TED tasks consists of much longer segments.

## 5 Experiment Results

### 5.1 Preliminary Check on Divergence Detection

The supervised classifier based on simple features yields competitive performance with published Cross-Lingual Textual Entailment results. On the 2012 test set, it achieves an accuracy of 60.4% , outperforming the best published result of 57% (Jimenez et al., 2012). On the harder 2013 test set, it achieves 43.6%, approaching the best published result of 45.8% (Zhao et al., 2013).

As a sanity check, we annotate a small sample of 100 randomly selected examples from Open-Subtitles. A bilingual speaker was asked to evaluate whether parallel segments in the two languages have exactly the same meaning or not. Surprisingly as many as 37% of examples were found to diverge in meaning. The nature of the divergences vary, but can generally be explained by discourse and explicitation effects (see Table 1).

The classifier detects semantically divergent

sentence pairs with a precision of 62.5% and a recall of 13.5%. The low recall shows that there is room to improve divergence detection, including by enriching the model, exploring alternate sources of supervision and adapting to the domain of the parallel data classified. Nevertheless, given that the default MT set-up consists in using all divergent sentences (i.e. detecting divergent sentences with a precision and recall of 0%), the current model represents a significant improvement.

### 5.2   Impact on Translation Quality

The learning curves (Figure 1) show that better translation quality can be achieved faster using NON-DIVERGENT as a selection criteria, even when compared to models trained on more data. On the validation set, the NON-DIVERGENT model achieves the BLEU score of the ALL model with only 60% of the updates.

RANDOM data selection yields a curve that is close to that of the ALL model. Selecting the first half of the corpus (NATURAL) plateaus about 6 points lower than the best models. The stark difference in performance between RANDOM and NATURAL might be explained by the fact that the RANDOM training set contains a more diverse set of sentences, sampled from a broader range of movies than the NATURAL dataset. This is supported by the corpus statistics in Table 2 which show that the RANDOM training set has a larger vocabulary size than the NATURAL one, especially in French. Training only on short sentences ($<$ 10 words) does much worse as the resulting system produces short translations which trigger high BLEU brevity penalties.

Table 3 shows the translation quality of the systems considered on two test sets using ensemble decoding. Following Sennrich et al. (2016a), translations are obtained by decoding with an ensemble of the 3 best models saved during training. The NON-DIVERGENCE criterion yields the best BLEU scores on both test sets, and even outperforms the system trained on all data by +1.6 BLEU on the MSLT task and by +0.6 BLEU on the TED task. System relative rankings are overall consistent with the learning curve: the NON-DIVERGENT system is best, either the ALL or RANDOM system are in 2nd or 3rd place depending on the test set, and using the NATURAL order of the corpus does much worse. Training on short sentences hurts in both cases, but particularly on the TED task which

| System | TED | MSLT |
|---|---|---|
| best mix (all data) | 33.03 | 40.11 |
| best mix (non-divergent) | 34.23 | 41.74 |
| + best model (all data) | **34.57** | **42.13** |

Table 5: Ensembles of systems (mix) trained on all data and non-divergent data yield modest improvements in BLEU

consists of longer segments.

### 5.3   Impact of Longer Training

One might wonder whether the trends above still hold when training longer, since training is expected to take longer to converge with more examples to learn from. We therefore continue training for all promising models (i.e. all but the system trained on short sentences only). Figure 5.3 shows that learning curves for NON-DIVERGENT, RANDOM and ALL eventually converge. However, Table 4 show that, among systems trained on the same number of examples, NON-DIVERGENCE remains the best data selection criterion, and that it yields decoding results that continue to outperform ensembles of models trained on ALL.

### 5.4   Ensembles of Models from Multiple Training Conditions

Finally, we evaluate whether models trained on ALL and on the NON-DIVERGENT data are complementary by augmenting the best performing systems in Table 4, which are all ensembles of models trained on non-divergent data, with the best model trained on the entire training set. Table 5 shows that the mixed ensemble improves over the previous best result by +0.34 BLEU on the TED test set and +0.40 on the MSLT test set. It is unclear whether these modest gains are worth the additional training time needed to add the ALL system to the mix. However, it remains to be seen whether better model selection could yield further improvements.

## 6   Related Work

**Translation Divergences**   Most prior work on translation divergences has focused on typological issues which reflect the fact that languages do not encode the same information in the same way. Dorr (1994) formalizes this problem by defining divergence categories (e.g., thematic, structural,

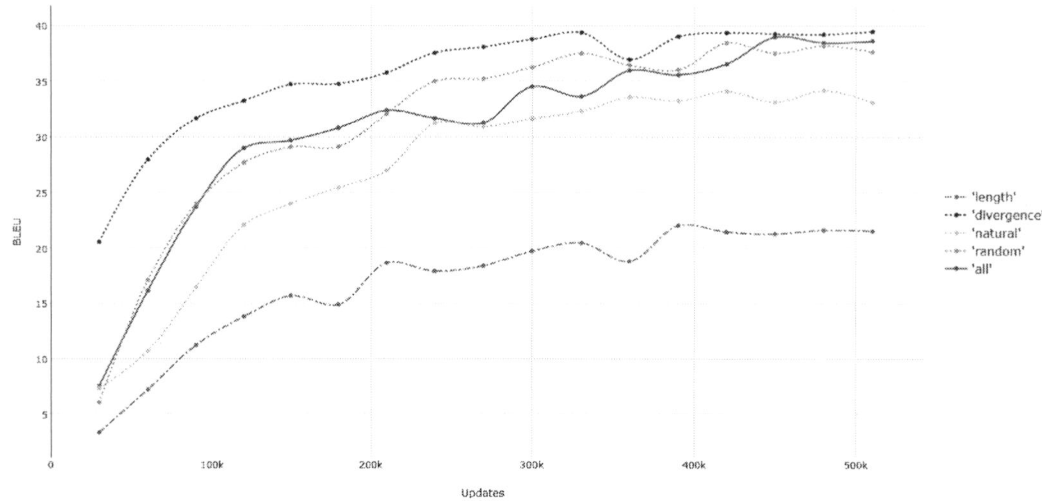

Figure 1: Learning curves on validation test set for all training configurations. Solid lines indicate a system trained on the entire training set, dotted lines use half of the training data with various selection criteria, and the dashed line indicates data selected by length. Training on the non-divergent half of the examples yields the top learning curve, even when compared to using all of the training data.

| Selected Data | Size (M) | TED | | MSLT | |
|---|---|---|---|---|---|
| | | 3-best | 3-last | 3-best | 3-last |
| non-divergent | 17 | **32.47** | **32.90** | **40.27** | **40.37** |
| random | 17 | 31.42 | 31.54 | 39.03 | 39.23 |
| natural order | 17 | 29.76 | 30.26 | 35.57 | 35.59 |
| length $< 10$ | 22 | 8.25 | 8.25 | 22.55 | 22.55 |
| all | 33.5 | 31.88 | 32.12 | 38.70 | 38.60 |

Table 3: Impact of data selection criterion on TED and MSLT test sets translated by an ensemble of the 3 best models saved during training. Filtering out DIVERGENT examples yields the best translation quality.

| Selected Data | Size (M) | TED | | MSLT | |
|---|---|---|---|---|---|
| | | 3-best | 3-last | 3-best | 3-last |
| non-divergent | 17 | **33.90** | **34.23** | **41.74** | **41.24** |
| random | 17 | 33.03 | 33.51 | 39.64 | 39.64 |
| natural order | 17 | 31.94 | 32.29 | 37.47 | 36.94 |
| all | 33.5 | 33.03 | 33.03 | 40.11 | 40.11 |

Table 4: Impact of longer training time on BLEU scores for TED and MSLT test sets translated by ensembles of 3 models. Filtering out divergent examples still yields the best translation quality, outperforming other selection criteria as well as systems trained on all data.

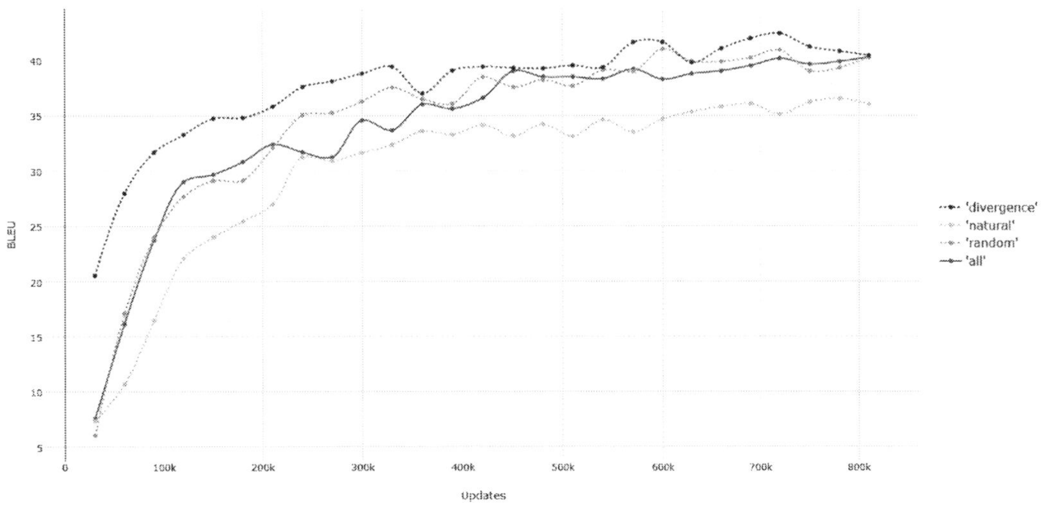


Figure 2: Longer learning curves on validation test set for most promising models. Training on NON-DIVERGENT examples remains the top system although RANDOM and ALL eventually converge to the same validation set performance.

categorical). Follow up work shows that divergences are not outliers but common phenomena in parallel corpora (Dorr et al., 2002; Habash and Dorr, 2002). Some of these divergences have been implicitly addressed by designing MT architectures informed by syntax and structure (Wu, 1997; Habash and Dorr, 2002; Chiang, 2007; Lavie, 2008, among others). In this work, we focused instead on semantic divergences which happen when the source and target sentences do not convey exactly the same meaning.

**Modeling Cross-Lingual Semantic Divergences**
Prior work has addressed cross-lingual semantic textual similarity (Agirre et al., 2016), entailment (Negri and Mehdad, 2010; Negri et al., 2012, 2013), translation quality estimation (Specia et al., 2010, 2016). While the human judgments obtained for each task differ, all tasks take inputs of the same form (two segments in two different languages) and output a prediction that can be interpreted as indicating whether they are equivalent in meaning or not. Models share core intuitions, relying either on MT to turn the cross-lingual task into its monolingual equivalent, or on features derived from MT components such as translation dictionaries and word alignments.

**Extracting Parallel Sentences from Non-Parallel Corpora** Extracting parallel sentences or parallel fragments from non-parallel corpora differs from our work in several ways. The goal is to identify additional training examples to augment parallel corpora, rather than to identify the most useful examples in a parallel corpus (Zhao and Vogel, 2002; Fung and Cheung, 2004; Munteanu and Marcu, 2005; Abdul-Rauf and Schwenk, 2009; Smith et al., 2010; Riesa and Marcu, 2012). The non-parallel examples tend to be more extreme than in the parallel corpora considered in our work.

**Data Cleaning** This line of work aims to remove noise, e.g., from alignment errors, based on scores from word alignment or language models (Okita et al., 2009; Jiang et al., 2010; Denkowski et al., 2012; Matthews et al., 2014). Cleaning training data in high-resource settings (Denkowski et al., 2012) and tuning data in lower resource settings (Matthews et al., 2014) has been shown to improve hierarchical phrase-based systems.

**Incorporating Word Alignments into Neural MT** Since our data selection criterion relies on word alignments, one could view our approach as part of the family of models that seek to improve neural machine translation using insights and models from word alignment and statistical machine translation models (Cohn et al., 2016; Mi et al., 2016). These approaches however focus on improving neural machine translation in low resource settings, while our aim was to identify a subset of examples in large training sets.

**Applications beyond MT** Detecting cross-lingual semantic divergences using entailment has been motivated by the need to synchronize content across languages in multilingual resources such as Wikipedia (Negri and Mehdad, 2010; Duh et al., 2013). It could also be useful to select better training examples for cross-lingual transfer learning of semantic models (Yarowsky et al., 2001; Ganchev and Das, 2013, among others).

## 7 Conclusion

We showed that neural machine translation is sensitive to semantically divergent parallel segments, as detected by a simple cross-lingual textual entailment system. When controlling for the number of training examples, filtering out divergent segments yields significantly better translation quality than using a random sample of examples, or short examples. Selecting non-divergent examples also improves translation quality compared to a system trained on twice as much data.

In future work, we will extend our empirical study to a broader range of tasks including more distant language pairs than English-French and a range of training domains in addition to subtitles. We will also evaluate whether our findings are impacted by the choice of optimizer, since it has been shown to have an impact on the initial performance and convergence of models on constant training data (Farajian et al., 2016). Furthermore, we will aim to answer two open questions raised by these promising results: can the cross-lingual entailment detector be replaced by a more direct approach for detecting divergence? And to what extent are alignment-based features useful when compared to neural models that might be closer to that of neural machine translation systems?

## Acknowledgments

We thank the CLIP lab at the University of Maryland and the reviewers for their constructive feedback. This work was supported in part by research awards from Amazon and Google.

## References

Sadaf Abdul-Rauf and Holger Schwenk. 2009. On the Use of Comparable Corpora to Improve SMT Performance. In *Proceedings of the 12th Conference of the European Chapter of the Association for Computational Linguistics*. Association for Computational Linguistics, Athens, Greece, EACL '09, pages 16–23.

Eneko Agirre, Carmen Banea, Daniel Cer, Mona Diab, Aitor Gonzalez-Agirre, Rada Mihalcea, German Rigau, and Janyce Wiebe. 2016. SemEval-2016 Task 1: Semantic Textual Similarity, Monolingual and Cross-Lingual Evaluation. In *Proceedings of the 10th International Workshop on Semantic Evaluation (SemEval-2016)*. Association for Computational Linguistics, San Diego, California, pages 497–511.

Amittai Axelrod, Xiaodong He, and Jianfeng Gao. 2011. Domain adaptation via pseudo in-domain data selection. In *Proceedings of the Conference on Empirical Methods in Natural Language Processing*. Association for Computational Linguistics, Edinburgh, United Kingdom, EMNLP '11, pages 355–362.

Dzmitry Bahdanau, Kyunghyun Cho, and Yoshua Bengio. 2015. Neural Machine Translation by Jointly Learning to Align and Translate. In *International Conference on Learning Representations (ICLR)*.

Yoshua Bengio, Jérôme Louradour, Ronan Collobert, and Jason Weston. 2009. Curriculum Learning. In *Proceedings of the 26th Annual International Conference on Machine Learning*. ACM, Montreal, Quebec, Canada, ICML '09, pages 41–48. https://doi.org/10.1145/1553374.1553380.

Ondrej Bojar, Rajen Chatterjee, Christian Federmann, Yvette Graham, Barry Haddow, Matthias Huck, Antonio Jimeno Yepes, Philipp Koehn, Varvara Logacheva, Christof Monz, and others. 2016. Findings of the 2016 conference on machine translation (WMT16). In *Proceedings of the First Conference on Machine Translation (WMT)*. volume 2, pages 131–198.

Mauro Cettolo, Christian Girardi, and Marcello Federico. 2012. Wit3: Web inventory of transcribed and translated talks. In *Proceedings of the 16th Conference of the European Association for Machine Translation (EAMT)*. volume 261, page 268.

Boxing Chen, Roland Kuhn, George Foster, Colin Cherry, and Fei Huang. 2016. Bilingual Methods for Adaptive Training Data Selection for Machine Translation. *Proceedings of the 12th Conference of the Association for Machine Translation in the Americas (AMTA)* page 93.

David Chiang. 2007. Hierarchical Phrase-Based Translation. *Computational Linguistics* 33(2):201–228.

Trevor Cohn, Cong Duy Vu Hoang, Ekaterina Vymolova, Kaisheng Yao, Chris Dyer, and Gholamreza Haffari. 2016. Incorporating Structural Alignment Biases into an Attentional Neural Translation Model. In *Proceedings of NAACL-HLT*. pages 876–885.

Michael Denkowski, Greg Hanneman, and Alon Lavie. 2012. The CMU-avenue French-English Translation System. In *Proceedings of the Seventh Workshop on Statistical Machine Translation*. Association for Computational Linguistics, Stroudsburg, PA, USA, WMT '12, pages 261–266.

Bonnie J. Dorr. 1994. Machine Translation Divergences: A Formal Description and Proposed Solution. *Computational Linguistics* 20(4):597–633.

Bonnie J. Dorr, Lisa Pearl, Rebecca Hwa, and Nizar Habash. 2002. DUSTer: A Method for Unraveling Cross-Language Divergences for Statistical Word-Level Alignment. In *Proceedings of the 5th Conference of the Association for Machine Translation in the Americas on Machine Translation: From Research to Real Users*. Springer-Verlag, London, UK, UK, AMTA '02, pages 31–43.

Kevin Duh, Ching-Man Au Yeung, Tomoharu Iwata, and Masaaki Nagata. 2013. Managing Information Disparity in Multilingual Document Collections. *ACM Trans. Speech Lang. Process.* 10(1):1:1–1:28. https://doi.org/10.1145/2442076.2442077.

Nadir Durrani, Fahim Dalvi, Hassan Sajjad, and Stephan Vogel. 2016. QCRI Machine Translation Systems for IWSLT 16. *International Workshop on Spoken Language Translation (IWSLT)* .

M. Amin Farajian, Rajen Chatterjee, Costanza Conforti, Shahab Jalalvand, Vevake Balaraman, Mattia A. Di Gangi, Duygu Ataman, Marco Turchi, Matteo Negri, and Marcello Federico. 2016. FBK's Neural Machine Translation Systems for IWSLT 2016. In *Proceedings of the Ninth International Workshop on Spoken Language Translation (IWSLT), Seattle, WA*.

Christian Federmann and William D. Lewis. 2016. Microsoft speech language translation (MSLT) corpus: The IWSLT 2016 release for English, French and German. In *International Workshop on Spoken Language Translation (IWSLT)*. Seattle, USA.

Victoria Fossum, Kevin Knight, and Steven Abney. 2008. Using syntax to improve word alignment precision for syntax-based machine translation. In *Proceedings of the Third Workshop on Statistical Machine Translation*. Columbus, Ohio, pages 44–52.

George Foster and Roland Kuhn. 2007. Mixture-model adaptation for SMT. In *Proceedings of the Second Workshop on Statistical Machine Translation*. Prague, Czech Republic, pages 128–135.

Pascale Fung and Percy Cheung. 2004. Multi-level Bootstrapping for Extracting Parallel Sentences from a Quasi-comparable Corpus. In *Proceedings of the 20th International Conference on Computational Linguistics*. Association for Computational Linguistics, Geneva, Switzerland, COLING '04. https://doi.org/10.3115/1220355.1220506.

Kuzman Ganchev and Dipanjan Das. 2013. Cross-Lingual Discriminative Learning of Sequence Models with Posterior Regularization. In *Proceedings of the 2013 Conference on Empirical Methods in Natural Language Processing*. Association for Computational Linguistics, Seattle, Washington, USA, pages 1996–2006.

Cyril Goutte, Marine Carpuat, and George Foster. 2012. The Impact of Sentence Alignment Errorson Phrase-Based Machine Translation Performance. In *Proceedings of AMTA-2012: The Tenth Biennial Conference of the Association for Machine Translation in the Americas*.

Nizar Habash and Bonnie Dorr. 2002. Handling translation divergences: Combining statistical and symbolic techniques in generation-heavy machine translation. In *Conference of the Association for Machine Translation in the Americas*. Springer, pages 84–93.

Silja Hildebrand and Stephan Vogel. 2013. MT Quality Estimation: The CMU System for WMT'13. In *Proceedings of the Eighth Workshop on Statistical Machine Translation*. pages 373–379.

Jie Jiang, Andy Way, and Julie Carson-Berndsen. 2010. Lattice score based data cleaning for phrase-based statistical machine translation. In *14th Annual Conference of the European Association for Machine Translation (EAMT)*.

Sergio Jimenez, Claudia Becerra, and Alexander Gelbukh. 2012. Soft Cardinality + ML: Learning Adaptive Similarity Functions for Cross-lingual Textual Entailment. In *Proceedings of the Sixth International Workshop on Semantic Evaluation (SemEval)*. Association for Computational Linguistics, Montreal, Canada, SemEval '12, pages 684–688.

Alon Lavie. 2008. Stat-XFER: A general search-based syntax-driven framework for machine translation. In *International Conference on Intelligent Text Processing and Computational Linguistics*. Springer, pages 362–375.

William Lewis, Christian Federmann, and Ying Xin. 2016. Applying Cross-Entropy Difference for Selecting Parallel Training Data from Publicly Available Sources for Conversational Machine Translation. In *International Workshop on Spoken Language Translation*.

Pierre Lison and Jörg Tiedemann. 2016. Opensubtitles2016: Extracting large parallel corpora from movie and tv subtitles. In *Proceedings of the 10th International Conference on Language Resources and Evaluation*.

Austin Matthews, Waleed Ammar, Archna Bhatia, Weston Feely, Greg Hanneman, Eva Schlinger, Swabha Swayamdipta, Yulia Tsvetkov, Alon Lavie, and Chris Dyer. 2014. The CMU Machine Translation Systems at WMT 2014. In *Proceedings of the Ninth Workshop on Statistical Machine Translation*. Association for Computational Linguistics, Baltimore, Maryland, USA, pages 142–149.

Yashar Mehdad, Matteo Negri, and Marcello Federico. 2010. Towards Cross-lingual Textual Entailment. In *Human Language Technologies: The 2010 Annual Conference of the North American Chapter of the Association for Computational Linguistics*. Association for Computational Linguistics, Los Angeles, California, HLT '10, pages 321–324.

Haitao Mi, Zhiguo Wang, and Abe Ittycheriah. 2016. Supervised Attentions for Neural Machine Translation. In *Prceedings of Empirical Methods in Natural Language Processing (EMNLP)*.

Dragos Stefan Munteanu and Daniel Marcu. 2005. Improving machine translation performance by exploiting non-parallel corpora. *Computational Linguistics* 31(4):477–504.

Dragos Stefan Munteanu and Daniel Marcu. 2006. Extracting Parallel Sub-sentential Fragments from Non-parallel Corpora. In *Proceedings of the 21st International Conference on Computational Linguistics and the 44th Annual Meeting of the Association for Computational Linguistics*. Association for Computational Linguistics, Sydney, Australia, ACL-44, pages 81–88. https://doi.org/10.3115/1220175.1220186.

Matteo Negri, Alessandro Marchetti, Yashar Mehdad, Luisa Bentivogli, and Danilo Giampiccolo. 2012. Semeval-2012 Task 8: Cross-lingual Textual Entailment for Content Synchronization. In *Proceedings of the First Joint Conference on Lexical and Computational Semantics - Volume 1: Proceedings of the Main Conference and the Shared Task, and Volume 2: Proceedings of the Sixth International Workshop on Semantic Evaluation*. Association for Computational Linguistics, Montr\?al, Canada, SemEval '12, pages 399–407.

Matteo Negri, Alessandro Marchetti, Yashar Mehdad, Luisa Bentivogli, and Danilo Giampiccolo. 2013. Semeval-2013 Task 8: Cross-lingual Textual Entailment for Content Synchronization. In *Second Joint Conference on Lexical and Computational Semantics (*SEM), Volume 2: Proceedings of the Seventh International Workshop on Semantic Evaluation (SemEval 2013)*. Association for Computational Linguistics, Atlanta, Georgia, USA, pages 25–33.

Matteo Negri and Yashar Mehdad. 2010. Creating a Bi-lingual Entailment Corpus Through Translations with Mechanical Turk: $100 for a 10-day Rush. In *Proceedings of the NAACL HLT 2010 Workshop on Creating Speech and Language Data with Amazon's Mechanical Turk*. Association for Computational Linguistics, Los Angeles, California, CSLDAMT '10, pages 212–216.

Tsuyoshi Okita, Sudip K. Naskar, and Andy Way. 2009. Noise reduction experiments in machine translation. In *ECML-PKDD, Proceedings of the European Conference on Machine Learning and Principles and Practice of Knowledge Discovery in Databases, Bled*.

Jason Riesa and Daniel Marcu. 2012. Automatic Parallel Fragment Extraction from Noisy Data. In *Proceedings of the 2012 Conference of the North American Chapter of the Association for Computational Linguistics: Human Language Technologies*. Association for Computational Linguistics, Montréal, Canada, pages 538–542.

Rico Sennrich, Orhan Firat, Kyunghyun Cho, Alexandra Birch, Barry Haddow, Julian Hitschler, Marcin Junczys-Dowmunt, Samuel Läubli, Antonio Valerio Miceli Barone, Jozef Mokry, and Maria Nadejde. 2017. Nematus: A Toolkit for Neural Machine Translation. In *Proceedings of the Demonstrations at the 15th Conference of the European Chapter of the Association for Computational Linguistics*.

Rico Sennrich, Barry Haddow, and Alexandra Birch. 2016a. Edinburgh Neural Machine Translation Systems for WMT 16. In *Proceddings of the 1st Conference on Machine Translation*. volume 2 Shared Task Papers.

Rico Sennrich, Barry Haddow, and Alexandra Birch. 2016b. Neural Machine Translation of Rare Words with Subword Units. *Proceedings of the Meeting of the Association for Computational Linguistics (ACL)* .

Jason R. Smith, Chris Quirk, and Kristina Toutanova. 2010. Extracting Parallel Sentences from Comparable Corpora Using Document Level Alignment. In *Human Language Technologies: The 2010 Annual Conference of the North American Chapter of the Association for Computational Linguistics*. Association for Computational Linguistics, Los Angeles, California, HLT '10, pages 403–411.

Lucia Specia, Varvara Logacheva, and Carolina Scarton. 2016. WMT16 Quality Estimation Shared Task Training and Development Data. LINDAT/CLARIN digital library at Institute of Formal and Applied Linguistics, Charles University in Prague.

Lucia Specia, Dhwaj Raj, and Marco Turchi. 2010. Machine translation evaluation versus quality estimation. *Machine Translation* 24(1):39–50. https://doi.org/10.1007/s10590-010-9077-2.

Jörg Tiedemann. 2007. Improved sentence alignment for movie subtitles. In *Recent Advances in Natural Language Processing (RANLP)*. volume 7.

Dekai Wu. 1997. Stochastic Inversion Transduction Grammars and Bilingual Parsing of Parallel Corpora. *Computational Linguistics* 23(3):377–404.

David Yarowsky, Grace Ngai, and Richard Wicentowski. 2001. Inducing Multilingual Text Analysis Tools via Robust Projection Across Aligned Corpora. In *Proceedings of the First International Conference on Human Language Technology Research*. San Diego, HLT '01, pages 1–8. https://doi.org/10.3115/1072133.1072187.

Matthew D. Zeiler. 2012. ADADELTA: An adaptive learning rate method. *arXiv preprint arXiv:1212.5701* .

Chiyuan Zhang, Samy Bengio, Moritz Hardt, Benjamin Recht, and Oriol Vinyals. 2017. Understanding deep learning requires rethinking generalization. In *Procedings of the International Conference on Learning Representations (ICLR)*. Toulon, France.

Bing Zhao and Stephan Vogel. 2002. Adaptive parallel sentences mining from web bilingual news collection. In *International Conference on Data Mining (ICDM)*. IEEE, pages 745–748.

Jiang Zhao, Man Lan, and Zheng-yu Niu. 2013. EC-NUCS: Recognizing cross-lingual textual entailment using multiple text similarity and text difference measures. In *Proceedings of the International Workshop on Semantic Evaluation (SemEval)*.

# Author Index


Al-Onaizan, Yaser, 56

Carpuat, Marine, 69
Chen, Boxing, 40
Cherry, Colin, 40
Cho, Eunah, 11

Denkowski, Michael, 18

Foster, George, 40
Freitag, Markus, 56

Goto, Isao, 47

Ha, Thanh-Le, 11

Knowles, Rebecca, 28
Koehn, Philipp, 28

Larkin, Samuel, 40

Morishita, Makoto, 61

Nakamura, Satoshi, 61
Nakayama, Hideki, 1
Neubig, Graham, 18, 61
Niehues, Jan, 11
Niu, Xing, 69

Oda, Yusuke, 61

Shu, Raphael, 1
Sudoh, Katsuhito, 61

Tanaka, Hideki, 47

Vyas, Yogarshi, 69

Waibel, Alex, 11

Yoshino, Koichiro, 61